PADDLING THROUGH THE STORMS

CHRISTI K. KASHA

PADDLING THROUGH THE STORMS
by Christi K. Kasha

www.thankyoufortoday.net

Copyright © 2011 by Christi K. Kasha

All rights reserved
This book or parts thereof may not be reproduced in any form, stored in retrieval system, or transmitted in any form by any means - electronic, mechanical, photocopy, recording, or otherwise - without prior written permission of the publisher, except as provided by United States of America copyright law.

ISBN-13: 978-0615477510
ISBN-10: 0615477518

Printed in the United States of America

Published by
▲Nacho Night▲
Media
Lilburn, Georgia

Cover by Scott Kent

Song reference Chapter 10: "If Tomorrow Never Comes," Garth Brooks, Garth Brooks © 1989 Capitol Records

Song reference Chapter 16: "Testify to Love," Wynona Judd Touched by an Angel Soundtrack © 1998 Sony BMG Music

Song reference Chapter 27: "Angels Among Us," Alabama Cheap Seats © 1993 BMG Entertainment

Book reference Chapter 29: The Power, Rhonda Byrne © 2010 Simon & Schuster

For
Ansley, my dream come true,
Faith, my prayer answered,
Kylee, my family complete,
The answer is nothing.

And for
Terry,
who truly is my better half,
because you loved me.
Thanks for asking.
And thank you for
yesterday, today, and tomorrow!

CONTENTS

Acknowledgements 6

The Storms

1. The Hope 9
2. The Truth 12
3. The Love Story 17
4. The First Storm 21
5. The Messages 39
6. The Answers 52
7. The Restorations and the Realizations 70
8. The Arrivals 78
9. The Second Storm 92
10. The Sun and the Rain 113
11. The Recovery 135
12. The Moments 144
13. The Confusion 153
14. The Lessons of the Game 158
15. The Fight 161
16. The Celebrations 168
17. The Choices 175

Paddling Through

18. The Understanding 183
19. The Paddles 188
20. The First and Ugliest Paddle 191

21.	The Paddle of Hope	198
22.	The Paddle of Fear	209
23.	The Paddle of Confidence	218
24.	The Most Beautiful Paddle	230
25.	The Paddle of Celebration	243
26.	The Paddle of Laughter	248
27.	The Paddle of Compassion	253
28.	The Paddle of Gratitude	263
29.	The Paddle of Perspective	273
30.	The Paddle of Action	281
31.	The Ongoing Pursuit of the Sun	292
32.	The Gifts	306

Acknowledgments

"Remember there's no such thing as a small act of kindness. Every act creates a ripple with no logical end."
- Scott Adams

My heart overflows with love and appreciation for the people who have been with me on this amazing journey. A special recognition and thank you:

To Terry, you've taken care of, supported, and believed in me. You looked after the girls and everything else with your endless patience and love, so I could follow my bliss. I couldn't have done this without you, nor would I have wanted to, and I'm not talking about just the book. There is no one that I would rather take this journey with than you. I love you, Sweetheart!

To Ansley, Faith, and Kylee, my incredible daughters, you couldn't be any more beautiful, inside or out, and I couldn't be any more proud of you! Your spirits and love fill each day with magical moments and joy. Being your mom is the most wonderful thing that I could ever do. You make my heart smile! I love all three of you so much!

To Bambi, the world would be a better place if everyone had a grandmother like you. Thank you for everything, but mostly for the security of your love. If you only knew how much you are loved…

To Dad, from you I get my passion for writing. May I honor you with it. I promise to remember what you have taught me, like to go for the next mailbox, to think outside of the box, and to keep in mind that

Jesus laughed. Your little girl is so proud that you are my father. I love you!

To Mom, you're the one who said that you envisioned me writing a book and you have been so supportive. Thank you for always encouraging us to dance. And thank you for what you have taught us through your examples, like putting family first, that working through a problem is worth the time and effort, and how to love unconditionally. I know that I can always call Mom. I love you, I love you, I love you!

To Bill, I always said that God knew I needed two dads. Thank you for accepting the job. I'm glad you had no idea of what you were getting into because our lives wouldn't be the same without you. You are loved deeply!

To Matt & Scott, my much adored brothers, you might be younger, but I look up to both of you. I credit you for the fun in this journey. You two are my heart and I'll always go get your bicycle back. I love you so much!

To Emily and Denise, my wonderful and crazy sisters-in-law, thank you for being who you are and for loving my brothers. You make our family complete.

To my nieces and nephews, always remember that you are loved.

Kenneth, I will never forget.

To Jim, Cheri, Myrna, Cindy, Donna, Kay, Susan, Judi, Meredith, Bob, the Kyles, and the Watkins, thank you for your examples of paddling with action and love.

To all of my Mountain View UMC family, thank you for bringing so much joy to my journey.

To Marjorie and Greg, thank you for your inspiration.

To Gale, thank you for the friendship, laughter, inspiration, and encouragement.

To Kim, your spirit is inspiring, your friendship treasured. I'm still trying to keep up with you!

To "my kids" of Mountain View, Hadley Farm and Little River neighborhoods, and Nicholson Elementary, you taught me more about life and love than I could ever teach you. There were days when it was you that I was paddling for. You are loved!

To the doctors and medical personnel who saved my life and kept my dreams alive, there is no way to adequately thank you. I can only promise that I will do my best to pay it forward.

To Marshall, thank you for rescuing me more times than I can count. I'm blessed to have you in my life!

To my Parkview and Berry friends, thank you for the magical moments!

To my mother-in-law and father-in-law, you raised in love the boy and then gave me the man. Thank you for such a wonderful gift!

To Dawn, thanks for the introduction! It changed my life and made this journey possible.

To all of the people who have impacted my life, from family, leaders, and my "other parents" to coaches, teachers, babysitters, and the man who held the door open with a smile, you have touched my heart and made a difference!

And to God, thank you for the joy, the miracles, and for replacing my sight with vision. Use me as you need me.

My gratitude and love to you all!

1

The Hope

"All my life I have tried to pluck a thistle and plant a flower where the flower would grow in thought and mind."
- Abraham Lincoln

There is no bitterness as I sit at my computer, typing mostly with just my right index finger, my back curved to bring my face close to the keyboard. Occasionally I will look up, my eyes hovering six or so inches away from the over-sized monitor where I can see well enough to scan for typos in the words that I have just punched out in a bold font that I have increased to twice the normal size. The constant nagging ache that starts in my left shoulder and runs all the way down my left side, past my hip and leg, and into my foot has intensified, so I decide that it's time to change positions. Concentrating on the motion and ignoring the pain, I move my forearm and hand from where they have been lying lifeless in my lap to the arm of the swivel office chair and stretch out my legs. I figure that I might as well go ahead and readjust my body in the chair as well and I release a preparatory sigh before lifting up. I'm all too aware that it will take more of a concerted effort than it normally does because of the weakness and pain left by the past weekend's flurry of activity. As I push up, the thought runs through my mind that it would make things so much easier if my left foot would just move the way it should. I make a mental note to be careful when I do get all the way up to leave the desk because odds are that my left leg will give me trouble. I recognize the feeling.

Settling back into the chair, relieved at my more comfortable position, I pause before once again lowering my face to the keyboard. I stare at the black characters suspended on their stark white background on the screen in front of me, wishing that they could somehow tell me, not only which words will best convey the message that I hope to share by writing this, but just what that message should really be. No, I'm not bitter. But I am somewhat apprehensive and nervous about my ability to transpose and relay that which I know to be true and which I feel certain someone needs to hear.

Perhaps my hesitation and nervousness are a result of my own questions of whether anything worthwhile really has come from the many years of tragedies, heartbreak, sadness, fear, and pain that I've been through. Or is the thought simply a coping mechanism that I've devised to have something positive to show for it all. Otherwise, it would mean that my suffering would have been for nothing. And that, I'm afraid, would be the one thing impossible for me to overcome.

But deep down I know that while I was going

through the storms of my life, I did discover something valuable. And it is something that I feel compelled to share because I realize that while I sit here, concentrating on typing, there are others who are focusing all that they have on just surviving, as I once was. However, the message that I want to affirm isn't simply a story about tragedy, heartbreak, sadness, fear, and pain, but of what those things revealed to me. It's a journey of survival and of discoveries. It is an account of how through the adversity, I explored and experienced moments of victory, an awareness of joy, the security of truth, and the comprehension of love. And with those discoveries came the proof that it hasn't all been for nothing, for in them there are meaningful and valuable lessons that are waiting to be used and passed along.

2

The Truth

God, grant me the serenity to accept the things I cannot change, the courage to change the things I can, and the wisdom to know the difference.
- Reinhold Niebuhr

Storms of adversity, they're out there. I've seen and experienced them firsthand. And if there is one thing that I've learned from them, it is that sometimes life just plain sucks. Well, it does. I wish that there was a way to get around that fact. Trust me, boy, do I wish! But, unfortunately, as long as we are sailing the vast oceans of life, there is a high probability that we will encounter some of those storms. When, where, and how they will come upon us is up to powers that are out of our control. How we navigate through them is our own personal choice.

The large majority of us, including yours truly, will deal with life's rough waters over and over again, in one form or another. Many of us will come to find out that life can be very hard at times, harder than we would have ever dreamed possible, worse than we would have thought we could bear. But even when life is rough, tough, unfair, and scary, there can still exist beauty and magic in it. Our nightmares can become fairy tales if we will keep in mind that even fairy tales have struggles, misfortunes, and hardships. It's the ending that counts. That's why I'm here.

In ways that are stranger than fiction and that have impacted my life and my family's lives forever, I have come to understand that the turbulent waters we encounter do not have to threaten our well-being or drag us down. In fact, we can use our storms, no matter how big or small, to lift us up, if we have the mindset to allow it. The currents caused by our storms can take us to places that we would have never reached otherwise. We can learn things about ourselves that we would have never known had it not been for the waves and the strong winds pushing us. And despite the pain and agony, we just might come away smiling and grateful.

If you are not currently experiencing some kind of adversity or if you have had the tremendous fortune of being one of the few who have never encountered the hardships that can blow our way, take a moment, right now, look upwards and shout, "Thank you!" Then continue along your journey with a smile on your face and appreciation in your heart.

But as you go, understand that life has a way of turning on a dime. I say that not to scare you, but oftentimes we don't place as much value as we should on the blessings we do have until something happens to make us stop and take notice. How much more would we appreciate the small joys in life if we thought that they might not be there tomorrow? When the skies overhead are a beautiful shade of blue and the clouds look like cotton balls, it's easy to forget that a sunny day can quickly turn stormy.

Would you like proof? I could share with you story after story of friends and loved ones who have been pounded by the adversity that blew into their lives completely unexpected. We could shake our heads in anguish and tear up together over their heartbreaks. Better yet, do your own research. Survey some of the people around you. Sit in a room with four or more people and odds are that at least one of them or a spouse has lost a job. Go talk to the father whose company had to close its doors last week. There is a new baby on the way. They were barely able to make ends meet as it was. What now? Sit with the mother who is settled in by her child's hospital bed, holding a precious little hand. She would give her life if he would just squeeze her's back. As she sits picking at the sandwich someone has thoughtfully brought her, she worries if anyone remembered that her older son at home needs poster board for his school project. Gosh, she misses him! Listen to the worries of the sweet little angel who often hears Mommy and Daddy fighting. She protectively holds a baby doll in her arms and a memory in her heart of them all laughing together. It's been so long. Will it ever be that way again? Try walking out in silence with the retired couple, holding hands as they leave the doctor's office after receiving the test results. The tears rolling down their faces as they quietly get into the car and drive away says more than words ever could. Yes, life can change quickly and it's not required to give us notice.

I pray that you never have to personally deal with true adversity. But most everyone will, at the very least, see threatening dark clouds ahead of him or her. For some people, the fear of what those dark clouds could bring, what could happen, what might take place is worse than any tragedy itself. Are you living each day so fearful of what could be looming in the distance that the beautiful, clear blue skies overhead are hardly noticed, much less appreciated? Do you sometimes almost wish that whatever horrible thing is lying in wait would just go ahead and happen? Then maybe the constant worry and dread would be over and you could be released to actually enjoy life.

Or are you reading this because you are one of the millions who have been hit by a storm of adversity and your life seems about as bleak as it can get? Do you feel as though you are drowning and it's taking all that you have just to keep your head above the water? You wait desperately for the clouds to part and for relief to come. "How long can I hold on?" you ask yourself, praying for help and scanning the horizon for the rescue boat that seems like it will never appear.

To you I say this, and I say it with everything that I have inside of me, "Don't you dare let go! Don't you even think about giving up!"

"Why not?" you ask, eager for even a shred of hope.

"Because I've been there... more than once," I

answer honestly. "I'm not writing this as a sideline lecture or pep talk that's meant to cheer you on. I'm writing it to share with you my story and the lessons I've learned through my experiences. I'm writing it to let you know that it is possible to come away from true adversity better and happier than you were when it came upon you. I'm writing it to tell you that you will survive!"

Let me follow that by saying that I have learned the hard way that no one can tell you the right way to paddle through a storm. You are the only one who can determine the best course for you. I can tell you my story, hoping that it will help you in some way, that it might give you some insights, but I can't write yours. I just wish to share with you that tough times can give us perspectives that we don't have on sunny days. They allow us to see that there can be joy in the middle of the pain, beauty in the darkness, and peace in the midst of the chaos. And they can teach us magical lessons about real happiness. I want you to know that it's worth the effort to paddle through those storms. So come with me through my journey, and perhaps along the way, we will discover something of yours as well. Grab your paddles and let's go!

3

The Love Story

*"If I ever had a choice,
my brain forgot to tell my heart."
- Christi Kasha*

"Thank you for today," I say to Terry, breaking the momentary quiet of our still, dark bedroom as we snuggle into our pillows.

"Thank you for today," comes my husband's reply, it's treasured predictability the reason for my smile.

"Good night, Sweetheart. I love you," I continue, my heart almost hurting from the weight of the truth behind the words.

"I love you, too. Good night, Sunshine." I smile again, thinking of the origin of his nickname for me, bestowed upon me twenty years ago, not as a compliment, but rather as a sarcastic comment on my morning disposition.

Rolling over onto my side, facing the outside of the bed, I feel Terry's strong hand come to rest on the curve of my waist. As I lay there absently focusing on the illumination of the street light shining in through the closed blinds, I hear, from down the hall, one of our girls stirring as she sleeps in the loft bed that her daddy built for her and that they painted together in her favorite colors of neon green and hot pink. My mind drifts to our other sleeping children and the day's activities, as well as those on the schedule for tomorrow. As I think of the hustle and bustle that consume our days, I mouth to God a silent, heartfelt "Thank you so much!" for the chance to live the life that I dreamed of. A mental journey begins through the blessings that have been given to me. Somewhere during my inventory of the last two years, I hear Terry start snoring beside me and I doze off, comforted by the sound.

Our nightly exchange of saying, "Thank you for today" and "I love you" to each other has been going on for nearly two decades, with only a handful of nights that it hasn't taken place. The only things that have broken our routine have been one of us being out of the country, an overnight stay where there was no phone service, the occasional all-nighters that I have pulled and, oh yeah, there was the coma.

We started it not long after we married. Terry and I were both watching a television show called Civil Wars, he in a hotel room somewhere in rural Alabama and me curled up on the sofa in our home in Atlanta. Terry traveled a lot back then and one of the ways we stayed connected was by watching our favorite television shows at the same time. Even if he was hundreds of miles away, it made me feel closer to him to know that we were still sharing something. This particular show's storyline focused on attorneys. On that night, one of their clients was an elderly woman. She told a main character, a female attorney, about how she and her late husband had, throughout their many years of marriage, ended each day by saying to each other, "Thank you for today." She went on to explain that there didn't have to be a special reason or anything out of the ordinary that had occurred during the day to invoke this exchange. It was just a reminder and an acknowledgement of their commitment and their belief that whatever happened or didn't happen that day, the important thing was that they had gotten to experience it together and that at the end of the day, they still had each other. As the show ended, the phone rang. It was Terry calling for the nightly phone conversation that we shared whenever he was out of town. This was back before cell phones and free long-distance calling, so we had the calling card number memorized and an hour's worth of time each weeknight figured into our monthly budget. The details of that evening's exchange were forgotten a long time ago, but its ending is still fresh in my mind. We were approaching the time to say good-bye, a time that I never did get used to, and the elderly lady's comments came to my mind. I thought that the act she described was so sweet and meaningful. I wondered if Terry had even noticed and, if so, what he thought of it. "Here goes nothing," I said to myself as I stood near the phone's cradle hanging on the wall. I was playing with the long blue cord, twisting it around my wrist, while working up my girlish nerve to risk looking foolish to the man that I so admired.

"Thank you for today." I held my breath

waiting for the reaction that I would receive.

On the other end of the phone there was a quiet laugh and then, "Thank you for today."

I must have been grinning like a schoolgirl with a crush. Yes, I had married the right man. He had not only picked up on this idea from the show, but he responded with heartfelt emotion. "I love you, Sweetheart," I told him. "Good night."

"I love you too, Sunshine. I'll talk to you tomorrow. Good night." The line went dead as he hung up. Terry was almost always the first to hang up. It was so difficult for me to break the connection between us. It would take many more years and a lot of experience with fear and pain and with laughter and love for me to fully appreciate the meaning behind the words we had just said and to understand that some connections just cannot be broken.

4

The First Storm

"Fear's strength is our weakness."
- Christi Kasha

It was the early part of December 1993 when the storm clouds started rolling in. I was enjoying life as much as any twenty-six-year-old could and having so much fun that I scarcely noticed the threatening elements. Barely out of our newlywed stage, Terry and I were excited about getting to spend a lot more time together during the rest of the year than we normally did. He wasn't scheduled for any out-of-town jobs and business at my mom and stepdad's sign manufacturing and installation company, where I worked in sales, was always slow in December. Since everyone lived in the metropolitan Atlanta area, we had enjoyed spending Thanksgiving with all of our family members. Now we were looking forward to kicking off the Christmas season with Terry's company's party. I had fun getting all dolled up in a semi-formal dress, Terry looked so handsome in his suit, and I couldn't wait to get to dance with him. The food and drinks would be plentiful, his co-workers were fun to hang out with, and the karaoke machine that had been brought in promised a lot of laughter for the evening. With the help of a few alcoholic beverages, I didn't hesitate to join some of the other wives in what was sure to be an award-winning rendition of "The Devil Went Down to Georgia" by the Charlie Daniels Band. We were already halfway through the first verse before I looked at the monitor in front of us. I realized that it was a good thing we had selected a song that I knew by heart because I couldn't read the words on the screen. I remember thinking, "I haven't had that much to drink. They should have a bigger monitor," as I made a mental note to get a better position directly in front next time. However, as my group was surprisingly not asked to give an encore performance, I thought nothing else about it and continued to enjoy the night.

It was several weeks later when I was lying in bed one night and looked at the alarm clock on the entertainment center against the opposite wall. It was intentionally placed on the other side of the room as a way to force me to get out of bed when it went off. Otherwise, the talent that I had developed for turning the alarm off, rolling over, and going back to sleep would be put into practice. But now its location was posing another challenge. I was shocked and confused to discover that I couldn't read the time it displayed. Blinking hard several times and then squinting did no good, I still couldn't read the lighted red numbers. I could see them, I just couldn't make out what they said. Finally, I resorted to crawling out from under the covers and down to the foot of the bed where I was half a room closer and could see the time.

As I lay back down and snuggled under the covers, the memory of the difficulty reading the karaoke words came to mind and I was more aggravated than worried. "Dang! I guess my near-sightedness has gotten worse," I complained silently. My previously diagnosed condition was so mild that I seldom used the glasses that I had. They spent much more time in a drawer at home than on me or even in my purse. Still, no one wants to think that his or her vision has deteriorated, even a little. "Oh, well. I need to go to the eye doctor for a checkup anyway. It's been forever." I put it on my mental to-do list, but didn't bother to mention the incidents to anyone as they didn't seem to be worth bringing up. It was the Christmas season and making an appointment kept moving farther and farther down the list.

The warm breezes of spring were in the air by the time I decided to deal with the reality that something was going on with my eyesight. It had been easy to ignore the trouble that I was having and to put off getting it checked out because whatever the problem was, it wasn't keeping me from actually being able to see things. It just made certain things blurry or hard to read, causing me only momentary trouble and inconveniences. But deep down I was beginning to suspect that something more significant that near-sightedness was wrong, and that's when fear and uncertainty took the place of busyness in keeping me from taking action. I didn't know what was wrong and wasn't sure if I wanted to find out. I was more scared of the diagnosis than I was of the struggles I was having. Fear can cause us to make decisions that aren't just illogical, but can be just plain dumb. I will always wonder how different the ending of this story might be if I had taken some sort of action, any action, immediately.

Instead, I let the weeks slide by, even though it was becoming harder and harder to brush off the difficulties that would pop up during the course of the day. I remember sitting at traffic lights and having a hard time seeing the turn arrows light up in their permission-giving green. Ordering what I knew was a good old stand-by at restaurants got me around having to struggle to read the menus. It also kept me from having to gauge if things were worse. Sometimes we try the hardest to hide the truth from ourselves. Then, if we're lucky, something happens that forces us to look at ourselves and face what is really going on.

One morning I was in the bathroom putting on my makeup while getting ready for work. To put my eye makeup on, I leaned so far over the counter that my breath fogged up the mirror in front of me. I felt the lump rise out of my tightened stomach and jump up into my throat as I realized that even at that distance, I couldn't see my eye clearly enough to apply the eyeliner that I was holding in my shaking hand. I took a deep breath, leaned back over, and ignored the look of worry on my face that was so obvious even I had no trouble seeing it. Even with this realization, I wasn't ready to give in just yet, so relying on my years of makeup applications and by glancing sideways, which allowed my peripheral vision to bring about some clarity, I finished my cosmetic routine to what I hoped was acceptable and wouldn't draw suspicion, and I left for work.

It's funny how when we reach a certain point, a minuscule amount of time can be all we need to go from inaction and indecisiveness to making significant adjustments and big decisions. By the time that I had driven the forty-five minutes to the other side of town where my office was, I had decided that it was time to do something; it was way past time, but better late than never. I recognized that I was scared and certainly wasn't feeling very courageous, so I knew that I needed to take some kind of action quickly, before I gave myself a reason to back out. I didn't have a regular eye doctor, but I remembered seeing a sign for one in a shopping center about a mile away from my office. Instead of turning right at the traffic light to go to work, I forced myself to continue straight ahead for a couple hundred feet and then to turn left into the center's parking lot. I copied the number off of the door, drove directly to my office, parked, walked purposefully to my desk where I picked up the phone and finally made the long overdue appointment. They were able to see me the next day. My method of coping was refusing to think about the appointment until that time came and I was forced to do so. "After all, it's just an eye exam," I told myself.

The next day and the appointment time came all too soon. The feeling in my stomach as I parked the car and walked in by myself is one that I have become way too familiar with in the years since. The apprehension, the fear, the concern were unnecessary, I told myself. And yet, I used those emotions to make this seem like an adventure of some sort, a challenge to overcome. "You can do this! " I coached myself.

I had told no one anything about this, not Terry, not my mother whom I saw every day at work, not my brothers whom I would trust with my life, no one. Perhaps keeping it to myself made it seem less real, and telling someone that I was worried there might be a problem was admitting that there might be a problem. Also, the secrecy gave me permission to handle it my way and to react however I wanted, without having to worry about someone else. At that moment, I needed to do what made it the easiest for me to cope, and privacy won out over support. That would come later, when it was really needed.

I made it inside and, in more ways than one, there was no turning back. After filling out the normal forms, I was taken to the exam room to meet with the optometrist. Though his name escapes me, I remember him as being extremely nice and the calming effect it had on me. The routine part of the exam didn't take long as we never made it past the first letter on the eye chart. No matter which eye I used or how many different lenses the doctor had me look through, I could not make out the large "E" at the top of the chart's triangle.

For someone who had always had close to

20/20 vision, this experience was beyond shocking, it was humiliating. I felt like I was doing something wrong. I felt like an idiot! Perhaps that is one of the reasons why I had waited so long before doing anything. Besides just wanting to ignore the problem, I didn't want to feel as though I was to blame in some way. It's funny how all too often, even when circumstances are out of our control, we get so busy blaming ourselves that we don't do the things that we do have control over. How much better would the decisions that we make for our lives be if we would just give ourselves a break once in awhile?

The doctor gave up and started a visual exam of my eyes by shining his penlight into one eye and then the other, again and again, at times pulling my eyelids open wider with his fingers. Finally, he put the light back in his shirt pocket and said in a calm, gentle voice, "Well, Christi, there's nothing wrong with your eyes. They look great." I sat in a stunned, confused, but relieved silence. He concluded his diagnosis. "I believe the trouble you are having is a nerve problem. Your optic nerve runs between your eyes and your brain. I think that is what is causing the problem. I'm going to refer you to a specialist to have it checked out." With those words began a journey for which I could have never prepared.

Back at work, I found my mother and told her that I needed to talk to her about something. We walked the couple of blocks up the road to the city park. I wanted more than anything not to have to tell her what was going on because I knew how upset and worried she would be, and yet instinct kicked in and got the upper hand. I was scared and threatened by something and I wanted my mother to protect me. We sat in the soft grass as I told her matter-of-factly that I had just come back from an appointment at the optometrist's because I had noticed that I was having some trouble with my eyes. I shared with her hesitantly the difficulties that I was experiencing. Then I went on to tell her what had happened with the exam and of the doctor's prognosis and referral. Mom was confused because it wasn't evident to an outsider that I was having any sort of trouble seeing. I did my best to explain that whatever was going on only made certain things hard to see and that most everything looked like it always had. It wasn't like I was losing my sight as if things were becoming dark. Some things just looked blurry. Mom was trying so hard to understand and I remember her pointing out the Coca-Cola vending machine fifty feet away from us and asking me if I could see it.

"Yep, I can see it," I answered, just beginning to discover how hard it can be to describe our physical senses and certain kinds of disabilities.

"What do you see or what does it look like?" she asked.

"Well, I can see the machine fine, but I can't really read anything on it."

"What about the white letters?" She was referring to the large Coca-Cola logo running sideways down the front of the machine. "Can you see or read them?"

"I can see them, but the only reason I know

what they say is because I recognize the shape and look of the logo." I'm a native Georgian, it would be a disgrace if I didn't recognize the Coca-Cola logo. "Other than that, I can't tell what anything else says."

"But you can see me... and the tennis courts over there... and the buildings... and the clouds...?"

I was nodding, but then cut her off. "Yes, Mom, I can see all of that. The details just aren't clear."

But the look on her face and the tears that started welling up in her eyes were all too clear, even for me. After all these years, remembering that look still hurts. It was the desperate, agonized look of a mother who, against those strong instincts, could do nothing to protect her child. I wonder how different her reaction would have been had she known at that moment what lay ahead.

In contrast, and strangely enough, I have no memory of breaking the news to Terry about my vision or the appointment, most likely because it was much less traumatic for me to do so. For one thing, my silence had already been broken, and often that first step is so much more difficult for us to take than all of the following ones combined. Perhaps we discover with the first one that whatever has been scaring us isn't as bad as we had feared. Another reason that I probably don't remember telling my husband the bad news is that there was no doubt in my mind how concerned and supportive he would be, but there weren't the same emotional strings that come with a mother and child relationship. However it happened, I explained everything to him and we made an appointment with Dr. Norton (not her real name), the specialist that the optometrist had referred me to. She was a neuro-ophthamologist, or a doctor who specializes in the nerves of the eye, practicing at Emory University Hospital, near downtown Atlanta.

I must have been a nervous wreck, but I also don't remember much about the days leading up to the appointment or the drive there with Terry and Mom. Looking back, I wonder whether my lack of memories is due to the fact that, while I was concerned about what was wrong, I had no idea that there was cause to be upset, or if I was coping by going into survival mode and putting myself on "automatic pilot." The emotional aspect might have been more than I could handle at that time. I needed information more than I needed anything else and that meant that I had to do this. The emotions could show up later.

What I do remember is waiting in the large, cold, sterile-looking waiting area, then Terry and I being taken back to the small, cramped exam room. Dr. Norton came in and introduced herself and the intern who would be sitting in on the consultation. She went through a battery of questions, some that I was expecting, some surprising. Then the tests started. When I once again couldn't read the top line on the eye chart, she moved on to the "How many fingers am I holding up?" test, followed by the "What color is the top of this marker?" test. After all of the probing questions were answered and the humiliating tests were completed, Dr. Norton, whom I strongly suspect had opted out of the "Bedside Manner with Patients" course in medical school, informed me in a no-nonsense manner that she did concur that there was some sort of problem with my optic nerve, that which sends messages from the eye to the brain. Although she could not say what it was, she could see that something had caused damage to the part of the nerve that controls my center field of vision, or whatever I look directly at. My peripheral vision fields, that which are off to the sides, the top, and bottom, had not been affected. Using those peripheral fields is how I was able to function in such a normal manner. Looking slightly to the side of whatever I wanted to see gave me more clarity, and I had been using that technique to compensate for the loss. But some things, such as reading, are extremely difficult without using central field vision.

The damage was severe enough that my visual acuity was not registering on the normal 20/20 type of chart and had fallen into the category referred to as "Counting Fingers," which is what the doctor was using when she asked if I could tell her how many fingers she was holding up. She went on to explain that this type of vision loss can be a symptom of Multiple Sclerosis, although it typically follows a different pattern with the person's vision returning on its own. An MRI, a picture of the brain similar to an x-ray, would show if I did have the disease. I was sent to another building of the hospital complex for the test. After checking in, I was given a gown to change into, then ushered to the room for the procedure. The technicians told me what to expect and explained that I needed to remain completely still and quiet during the test. I lay down on the rolling table and they slid me into the machine. Since I would be completely inside the dark, tunnel-like hole, they gave me a button to push if I started feeling claustrophobic. The test wasn't bad, just long and boring. There was nothing to do but listen to the ongoing metallic tapping sound made by the machine as it took pictures of the inside of my head.

Afterwards, we returned to the doctor's office and waited as the MRI films were read. Then, in that stupid little clinical-feeling room that made it feel as though my world really was closing in on me, with that stupid eye chart hanging on the wall in front of me as if it were mocking me, and the doctor wearing that stupid white lab coat as though she was somehow deserving of protection from threatening elements, I felt the full impact of the storm come crashing in on me. It hit full force as Dr. Norton said, "The results from the MRI show no evidence of Multiple Sclerosis. While that's good, with MS, a patient's vision usually returns on its own after a short time. But since you don't have MS, there isn't anything that I can do to treat this. I don't think that your eyesight is going to improve, but I don't think that it will get any worse either. Because it is a nerve problem and doesn't have anything to do with your eyes, glasses or contacts won't do any good. I'm sorry about that." As she stood up to get her files together, she nonchalantly asked, "You're not driving, are you?"

"Yes, I have been," I answered meekly.

"Well, of course you can't do that anymore."

I felt like I was drowning and the person who was supposed to be my rescuer had just turned on me and was driving off with the only boat there was.

"I'll send your paperwork up to the checkout desk. Come back in to see me if anything changes," There was no emotion in her voice.

"The hell I will!" I screamed inside while fighting back the tears.

She walked out of the exam room, and I was convinced that she was on her way to destroy her next patient's life. I could hardly stand to look at Terry, although I desperately needed to see some evidence of his love for me. I was scared that instead I might see some sort of disappointment in or resentment towards me. Once again, I felt as though I had done something wrong and that I was letting everyone down. But, not being able to help myself, I glanced at my husband. What I saw was compassion all over his face, and the love that I needed to see was pouring from his eyes. If we said anything to each other, I don't remember what it was. But I doubt that words were needed. The looks on our faces said it all.

It was then that the dark-haired, nice-looking young intern spoke up for the first time. He had been sitting on a rolling stool, observing, but off to the side. The warm look had never left his face. With the doctor out of the room, I suppose he felt that it was okay to address me. Seeing the couple of tears that had escaped from my eyes, he said to me in a voice filled with sympathy, "I'm so sorry, Mrs. Kasha. Those things that you do everyday without thinking about them are usually the hardest to give up. But, you'll be okay. You really will. You'll see." What a difference his simple comment made at one of the worst moments of my life. I will never forget it and have always wished that I had a way to thank him. Two doctors in the room, one focused on my physical handicap, the other took the time to address my emotional needs. One diagnosed me, the other helped me get started down the path of healing.

As we left the exam room and were walking down the hall, I heard the doctor's voice coming from behind me. I turned and looked back over my shoulder. She was sitting at her desk, making verbal notes into a hand-held recorder, the door wide open. "Patient #36194, 26-year-old female, experiencing central field loss, no history of...." Her voice trailed off behind me as I walked out. I could not remember ever feeling as hopeless as I did at that moment. Then I realized that I had a chance; love stood beside me clasping my hand in his to let me know that I could borrow the strength I needed from him.

Mom was anxiously waiting for us near the reception desk as we reentered the waiting area. Terry did most of the talking as we relayed what the doctor had told us. Mom hugged me, not even trying to fight back her tears, and the three of us walked out in near silence. The drive home and the rest of the day are a complete blur.

I didn't think that it was possible, but the next morning the sun came up! I figured that if the world was going to go on in the middle of my agony, then I might as well do the same. After showering and getting dressed, I went to work. Yes, I had heard the doctor's instructions about not driving, but I was in survival mode and needed time to come to terms with this news. My vision was not any worse that day than it had been the week before and I wasn't having trouble driving then. For some reason, Terry did not put up a fuss. Whether that came as a result of trust that I knew my own limits, the same logic that I was using, or his gut reaction to give me some space, I can't say. However, much to my surprise, my other family members would follow suit. Perhaps it was because we were all in shock over the news, or more likely, the lack of resistance stemmed from the fact that I seemed fine and the vision loss had not altered my life in any drastic sense. Later I would learn that nobody had any idea of what a significant problem it was and how many things it affected. "You hid it well," I've been told.

During the six months since I had first noticed a problem, I had continued selling signs all over the metropolitan Atlanta area, putting on an average of two thousand miles a month on my new car. The job required measurements, material and color selections, pricing, drawings, and work orders, and I had kept doing all of those things. Well, I would fall behind in writing up my work orders, but that had nothing to do with my eyesight. It was paperwork and it was boring. Terry still traveled a lot while I worked, taught children's classes at church, and held down the home front. You would have never been able to tell that there was anything unusual about our circumstances. Even the sightseeing vacation that we took to the Pacific Northwest posed very few challenges, although I do wonder, looking back, how many of the sights were even more breathtaking than I realized.

There were many, many things that were either impossible or hard for me to do, but I just learned to adapt. For example, when I was worried about seeing a turn arrow at an intersection, I followed the other cars' lead or watched the cars across from me turning in the opposite direction to know when the turn arrows were activated. If it was a busy or unfamiliar intersection, I would turn right onto the cross street and then turn around so that I would be going straight across at the light. But the easiest thing was just to take routes where this wouldn't be a problem. My driving philosophy: better safe than sorry, nothing wrong in waiting.

I carried a magnifying glass in my purse at all times to read small print. If I couldn't make out specific product or color codes while at a sales appointment, I would make other notes such as "third one down on page two," then use my magnifying glass to find the correct code when I got back to my car. And, to be completely honest,

I got very good at lying to get myself out of sticky situations. "Oh, I already put your card in my purse. Would you mind telling me your company's name again?" I might say. Besides the embarrassment of having a physical handicap, I was scared that I would lose business that our small company needed if potential customers thought that I wasn't capable of handling their orders or because of the prejudices that many people have towards the handicapped.

More than anything, I adapted by learning to rely on my peripheral vision. The central field vision loss, I explained to my family, amounted to a blurry spot about the size of a large thumbprint in the center of wherever I looked. Everything else was completely clear. So, for example, if I was sitting across from my brother at a table and looked at his eye, it would appear as if someone had smudged it, but if I looked to the side just a little, I could see it clearly.

The whole thing was strange and very hard to explain. I remember my mother on more than one occasion saying to me, "I just don't get it. You can't see those large letters on that sign, but you can see tiny stars millions of miles away or that little-bitty ant crawling on the ground. It doesn't make sense."

"No, Mom. It doesn't," I cried out silently.

I might have adapted the most by using my peripheral vision, but I adjusted by getting tough. I learned to not let someone honking or riding my bumper get to me, I tuned out to the looks that people gave me, I tried to ignore my disability when I could, and when I had no choice, I just sucked it up. It was never a matter of it not being embarrassing, difficult, or sad for me, but this storm had stolen some of my sight. I wasn't going to let it take away my happiness or any of the meaning I had for my life. So I paddled on.

5

The Messages

*"The greatest messages may be heard with our
ears and seen with our eyes,
but they are received by our hearts."
- Christi Kasha*

About eight months later the skies overhead grew darker when the first fender bender happened. Although my confidence was shaken and I was forced to rethink my circumstances, to this day I stand by the belief that my eyesight was not a factor. It was technically my fault, but it occurred on one of those busy roads where normal traffic conditions are horrendous. I had been involved in a similar fender bender five years before that and a co-worker had an accident just a month earlier, both at almost the exact same spot. This one was so minor that the police officer didn't even issue a citation. The other driver was not as understanding. She was furious because she was on her way to a bar and I was making her run late.

The next mishap, however, I didn't get off so lucky. I was given a ticket for following too close, which translated meant that the lady in front of me slowed down as she was turning more than I did.

It could have been that I was simply paying too much attention to something on the radio, but I had to admit, at least to myself, that it was possible that I couldn't see her brake lights in time. She was very sweet and nobody was hurt. The hood had buckled on my car, but at least it was drivable. I, on the other hand, was a mess. I couldn't get around having to consider the fact that my vision might have caused this. I didn't want to quit driving, but that nice lady could have been hurt. Maybe it would have happened anyway, maybe it was just a bad coincidence, maybe not. I was going to have to rethink and revisit all of the decisions that I had made about how to deal with my problem and that wasn't going to be easy. There was so much on the line no matter what course I chose, and the dark clouds enveloped the sky in every direction.

For the next several days I stuck close to the office on roads that I was extremely familiar with. I was in torment when I went to a sales appointment at a retirement center a few miles away. I parked my car with its smashed hood in a parking space near the front entrance. Carrying my briefcase and some samples, I was walking in when an elderly lady said hello. I assumed that she was a resident who had come outside to sit on the front patio where she could enjoy the unusually warm weather for January. I returned her greeting and gave her a smile that I hoped revealed my appreciation for her friendliness. Standing up slowly and walking towards me, she asked sweetly, "Honey, what happened to your car? You're okay, aren't you?"

"Yes, ma'am. I had a little wreck the other day. Thankfully no one was hurt and it was my car that had the most damage. I just haven't gotten it fixed yet."

She responded in a voice that held a heavenly tone unlike anything that I had ever heard before or since, "This too will pass. Just remember that all things work together for good for those who love Him." That and nothing more.

"I sure will. Thank you."

Her sweet smile and the slight nod of her head spoke volumes to my heart on compassion and faith. With a couple of pats to my shoulder, she returned to her seat. I continued inside to the appointment. It went well, but somehow I don't believe that my reason for being there that day had anything to do with signs, well, signs for the building and its grounds, that is.

Before leaving, I looked all around the center's common areas for "my angel," as I refer to her. She wasn't in any of the places that I could visit and not knowing her name, there was nothing more that I could do. I went to my car and found a turning point in my life waiting there for me.

Sitting down in the driver's seat, I put the keys in the ignition, but my hand hesitated before starting the engine. My mind was focused on the lady's words and the way she had said them, not as though she were quoting Bible verses, but as if she was actually relaying a message to me. Those words that I had heard so many, many times before, words of trust and faith and hope, had just found their way into my personal situation and had taken on a whole new meaning. With that realization, the tears began. Tears that had been held back for fourteen months found their way to freedom, tears of fear and sadness, tears for the disappointment and the frustration, tears for all of my embarrassment and my regrets, and tears of uncertainty and knowledge. I sat there in the parking lot of that retirement center, sobbing, for how long I do not know. But I cried uncontrollably for anything and everything, for dreams lost and for miracles desired, for not knowing what would happen and for knowing what I had to do. I cried out of anger and out of self-pity, I cried because no one understood and because I had so much support. Sitting there, I had never felt more alone, and yet somehow I sensed that I wasn't.

As the tears began to subside, I found myself praying, "Please, God...," not even knowing how to verbalize all that was going through my mind. I had to trust that He knew because I'm not sure that I did. The story of Jesus healing the blind man by putting His spit into the man's eyes came to my mind. There was no one around to see how crazy I was and I thought that maybe if God just saw that I had faith, He would heal me too. I told God that I knew that in the story it was Jesus' saliva, but maybe He could use His Spirit through mine. I spit into my palms and rubbed in into my eyes, then closed them tight. I let a couple of minutes pass while I sang a few of my favorite spiritual praise songs. Finally I opened my eyes and looked at the world outside my car. There was no change, or so I thought. "No miracle today, I guess. Oh well, that's okay," I said to myself with disappointed sincerity and the tiniest of smiles on my face. My hand once again came to rest on the keys in the ignition. This time they were turned. I pulled out of my parking space and as I drove out of the lot, I sent a silent, "Thank you," out to my angel, wherever she might be.

I realized that part of what was hard to grasp about this whole thing was that when I asked God, myself, or the universe, "What did I do to deserve this?" the answer was "Nothing." When I asked, "Did I do something to cause it?" I heard, "No." When I questioned, "Is there some reason for this?" I didn't get any response at all. Knowing that I didn't deserve or cause this to happen should have been reassuring. The problem was that the answers also pointed out the lack of control that I had over what was happening to me. As I sat there thinking about what I had been told, I realized that the words, "and this too shall pass" might not have been spoken simply about the hassles that come from being involved in a car accident. Maybe they were meant as a message about my eyes and the physical and emotional struggles that I was coping with, but I also knew that nothing could pass, physically or emotionally, unless I dealt with it. While I might not be able to change the circumstances, I did have a certain kind of control over the outcome of this storm. It was time to chart the course that I wanted to take. And with my decisions would come the answer to,

"Is there some reason for this?" What that answer would be remained to be seen.

I eased my way back to my office, went inside and sat down at my desk, which was just inside the front door. In the bottom drawer, I located a copy of our insurance company's authorized providers. I searched and found the name of another neuro-ophthalmologist in Atlanta. It was hard to read the phone number that was in such small print, but with my magnifying glass, I was able to decipher one number at a time. It was the numbers that were shaped very much alike that gave me the most trouble, 6's, 8's and 3's for example, or 1's and 7's. Finally I had copied down what I thought was correct, at least it was enough digits to make up a complete phone number. I picked up the receiver and seeing that someone was on line one, I pressed the button for line two, heard the dial tone, and pushed the numbers. When the sweet voice of the office administrator answered, I explained that I had been told by Dr. Norton at Emory that I had central field vision loss because of optical nerve damage. I went on to explain that she had predicted that it wouldn't get any worse, but I was pretty sure it had and that I would like to see another doctor.

"Well, let's get you in as soon as we can so that Dr. Weiner can examine you and see what we need to do," she said confidently and reassuringly. I felt a small glimmer of hope and wondered if maybe she was related to the intern at Dr. Norton's office. After hanging up, I called Terry, who thankfully was in town that day and could be easily reached by phone. "Hey, I wanted to let you know that I just made an appointment with another neuro-ophthalmologist. I'm scared that my eyes have gotten worse, so I need to get it checked out, but I want to try another doctor."

"Christi, if you think you need to go, then let's get you in."

"I've got an appointment on Thursday at 11:00 with Dr. Nancy Weiner. She's on our insurance plan and she's beside Piedmont Hospital. Can you go?"

"You couldn't stop me."

"Thanks, Sweetheart." I was comforted to hear what I already knew would be the answer. "I love you so much! I'll see you at home." Then I threw in before hanging up, "Remind me to tell you about an interesting sales appointment that I had today," as if I'd forget.

Later that day, as we sat together on the sofa, I would tell him about "my angel" and what she had said to me. But the tears that I had cried, the prayer, and the attempt to heal my own eyes would remain between God and me for awhile longer, as in several more years. It wasn't that I didn't think Terry would understand or that he would think I was being silly; in fact, just the opposite would have been true. I simply wasn't ready to let anyone in on how upset and desperate I was yet, although I'm sure they could have guessed. But knowing that I was causing more concern and sadness for the people I loved was more than I could handle right then. I knew that they were there for me if I wanted to talk, but parts of this journey, I needed to paddle solo.

As soon as I hung up with Terry, I went to tell Mom what was going on. I told her about how I was worried that my eyes had gotten worse, not just because of the accidents, but that I had noticed some other minor things as well. I told her about the appointment with the new doctor.

"I'm glad you're going." Then hesitantly, she said, "I've been getting a little worried because I've noticed some small differences too."

"You have?"

"Well, it seemed like it, but I was waiting to see if I was just more tuned into what you are not able to do."

"Like what?" I asked hesitantly, not sure if I really wanted to know.

"The main thing is that your writing on work orders and other paperwork doesn't seem as neat and is harder to read."

Part of me wished that I hadn't asked. I needed to know, but I had always been complimented on my neat handwriting and even though it was something insignificant, I was proud of it. This was just one more thing that had been taken away from me. Most of us are insecure enough that we try to hold on to anything and everything that we see as giving us merit and setting us apart, even in the most minor of ways.

"Mom..." I started off, but then stopped. Every muscle in my body had tightened up and my breathing was labored. I remember thinking to myself, "If I can just get the words out, it will be over." I tried again. "Mom, I've decided that I need to stop driving." There, it was done. The decision was made. I didn't get upset or cry. I was past that point. The emotions had come before the verbalization, now there was an almost eerie sense of relief.

Mom wrapped her arms around me and pulled me close. "Oh, Honey, I think you are making the right decision, but I know this is killing you. Keep in mind that it might not be forever."

"Yeah, right," I thought.

"You know that I'll help in any way that I can," she promised. That I knew I could take to the bank.

Still, I was painfully aware that the joy and freedom I had always gotten from being behind the wheel was something that even Mom's treasured love wouldn't be able to replace. This was the hardest decision that I had ever made. It wasn't just a matter of it making things more difficult and stopping me from being able to go wherever I wanted, whenever I wanted. That would be a huge adjustment, yes, but what was now causing me the most agony was that I absolutely loved driving, I always had, and now I was being forced to give that up. For me, this was worse than the vision loss itself. That's one of the greatest dangers with life's storms. The damage that they often cause isn't the trouble and the struggles that they bring into our lives, but the happiness and harmony that they steal from us.

I drove myself home that afternoon, knowing that it would most likely be my last time behind the wheel. The radio was tuned to my favorite station and I had it cranked up like a teenager on a Saturday night. I relished every minute of the bumper-to-bumper rush hour traffic because it gave me that much longer to drive. Never had I been more thankful to see so many cars on the Interstate highways. The traffic might have been heavy, but surprisingly, my heart felt lighter than it had in a long time. The decision might have been painful, but having it hover over me had been emotionally exhausting.

And the best part of it was that when I quit putting off something that I dreaded, I began seeing so much more. I started learning that all things can work together for good. Oh, if I had only known then just how true that would end up to be, I would have taken action so much sooner! Looking back, I see that that day was an ending to some things in my life, but it was also a starting point for others.

I lost and I found things. I made decisions to let some things go and to take control of others. I gave up driving, but I began to understand that, although my vision may not have been restored in that parking lot, a healing had begun. In exchange for no longer hiding my fears, I found out, through Mom, Terry, and even that nice intern, that the most precious kind of help has nothing to do with being able to fix a problem and everything to do with being there for someone as they are dealing with it. A stranger reached out to me when I was in need of hope. Her words were nothing profound or new, but spoken at the right time and in the right way, I was able to hear what

I needed to hear. She gave me a valuable message, but taught me something even more important about giving as well as receiving. I learned firsthand that kind, uplifting words spoken to strangers just might have a greater impact on their lives than we will ever know. I found out that what we need can come at the strangest times and in the strangest places. Being at the retirement center when all of this happened gave me the time and the privacy to let it all out. My breakdown was painful, but it let me discover that tears are one of God's greatest gifts.

That day, through my weakness, as the tears streamed down my face, I found the strength to make some tough decisions. Maybe it was that a good cry has a way of clearing our minds and giving us a fresh start or maybe I was so empty from sobbing and releasing all of the fear, the uncertainty, and the pain that I had no choice but to reach out and reach up. And in doing so, I discovered that a small, but brave, step in faith can launch you forward towards the sun.

And a brave step it was, going to the appointment with the new doctor. I dreaded the embarrassment, the frustration, and the despair that I had felt after the last two exams. Who in their right mind would want to go through that again? It's hard to explain, but there is something horrifying about finding out what you can't do. That feeling was there in my stomach again and it took everything I had to make myself walk in the door that Terry was holding open for me. But onc I did, it wasn't long before I discovered that worrying about this appointment had been a waste of emotional energy. Immediately, I picked up on the differences- the waiting area was small and cozy, the sweet lady that I had made the appointment with was as nice in person as she was over the phone, and Dr. Weiner came out to the waiting room, introduced herself with a smile, and walked us back to the large exam room herself. I had a feeling from her warm, friendly smile that I wouldn't be hearing her refer to me as a number. By the end of the appointment, I was convinced that she had received an A+ in that Bedside Manners course, the one that the other doctor opted out of. Lesson learned: different people, different circumstances, different experiences. Though her diagnosis was the same - optic neuritis with central field vision loss, or in layman's terms, damage to the optic nerve causing a "blind," or blurry, spot in the center of my vision, with no known cause, vision measuring Counting Fingers - her demeanor and attitude were like a life preserver being thrown to me.

"Well, I'm not sure what's going on here, but we are going to do everything we can to figure it out," Dr. Weiner reassured me. "The first thing we need to do is get you in for another MRI. Now, let me tell you what I'm thinking. One of the things that this might be is Multiple Sclerosis. I know that the MRI you already had didn't show that you have MS, but it's possible that it was in the very early stages then and it might show up now. Your symptoms don't fit its normal pattern, but you never know how a disease like that might present itself. I'd rather let the MRI tell us for sure. The other thing that could be causing this is going to sound scarier than it is. I don't want you to get too worried because it would be fairly easy to fix with surgery. I want to check for a pituitary brain tumor. It would not be cancerous and they are not uncommon, and again the last MRI might not have detected it if it was very small then. It could be that you have one that's putting pressure on your optic nerve. Like I said, it can be surgically removed and then your vision should come back. If that's what it is, it will show up on the MRI as well. So, that's where we need to start."

"Let's start," I smiled, just thrilled to be doing something! The test was scheduled for several days later.

Life is truly a matter of perspective. Who would have ever thought that being told you might have a brain tumor would bring some kind of welcomed relief? It was at least a diagnosis, and one with a positive outcome. I was so tired of not knowing. Sometimes no news isn't so good. I left the building with the possibility of finding out what was wrong and with a huge smile on my face. Perhaps my life wasn't over. Or was it?

6

The Answers

"Come to the edge, he said.
They said, we are afraid.
Come to the edge, he said.
They came. He pushed them.
And they flew..."
- Guillaume Apollinaire

As the day of the MRI approached, those two words "brain tumor" began to seem more and more ominous. The night before the test, I hardly slept at all. I lay awake thinking of what might be yet to come. Every emotion that I had ever felt came back to me as I tossed and turned. With morning came the drive to the hospital. Terry just held my hand most of the way and we listened to the radio. Once again, I changed into a gown and listened to the instructions. Perhaps because I knew what to expect with the test, my mind was focused more on the results that would come from it. As the equipment was being prepared, I sat nervously on the end of the table and I did the only thing that I could do, I said a quiet, simple prayer. There were no fancy words, no long drawn out pleas, just one heartbreaking request, "God, I just want to know if I'm going to die.

Please, just let me know if I'm going to die."

Thirty long seconds later, the technicians told me to go ahead and lie back. They reminded me to let them know if I started feeling claustrophobic. As I thanked them, I thought to myself, "I wish that that was my biggest concern." I was rolled into the giant machine that represented judge and jury to me. The loud, metallic sounding, tapping noise indicated that the test was underway. I closed my eyes and lay completely still as instructed. Although the noise inside was constant and loud, I was exhausted, not only from the lack of sleep the night before, but also from the fatigue that stress and fear can cause. I fell asleep.

There is no way to prove to myself or others what it was that happened next, but I have always called it my vision from God. It could be classified as a dream or given some other scientific explanation, but call it what you will, the result was still the same. It was an answer to my feeble prayer, whispered during the storm.

Suddenly, I was standing in total darkness with nothing above, below, or around me. Then directly above me, two semicircular doors appeared and began parting as if I had been waiting for a round elevator on the ceiling. As they slid open, a brilliant light of the purest white poured out. The beauty of it is indescribable and gave me the same kind of feeling as when you see a sunset that takes your breath away and stirs something deep within you, and yet you know that its colors can never be adequately explained with words. As I stood there looking into the light, I could see that there was someone standing above me, just to the side of the opening. It was a shadowy silhouette of a man. I knew instinctively that it was Jesus.

He looked down at me and sweetly spoke just two words, "Not yet."

Then the doors above me began to close and I watched the light disappear behind them. My heart broke as I realized that the answer I had just received, the one I so desperately wanted, meant that, at least for the time being, I wouldn't be able to experience the feeling I had gotten from seeing that light and from standing there near Jesus. The emotions I felt as those doors closed were completely unexpected and unexplainable. All I can say is that they are the reason that I know this was something more than just a dream. Yes, I had gotten the answer that I had begged for, but it left me feeling sad and devastated. Suddenly all of the dreams that I had for myself and my future- being with Terry, having children, enjoying life- paled in comparison to the spirituality that I had just been a part of. I didn't want it to end, no matter what it meant that I'd be giving up.

As human beings, our natural instinct is to fight off death. While I would still fight with everything I have for my own life, for the lives of my loved ones, and hopefully for anyone's, never again will I have the same sort of fear or sadness over dying as I did before that experience. It was beautiful and it was love.

Then I woke up and realized where I was. Still very emotional from what had just taken place, I was more than happy to lie there with my thoughts for the few more minutes that it took to finish the test. Once it was completed, I was rolled out of the machine. "Everything went well. We can't discuss any of the results with you," one of the technicians told me as he helped me down off the table. "A doctor will review the films and someone will call you within a week with the results."

"Within a week? I can't wait that long! How about tomorrow?" I thought. But wait I did.

Thankfully, it just so happened that I had scheduled this test right before Terry and I were leaving for a visit to the New England states. Terry had to go for a short business trip, and since neither of us had been to that part of the country, we decided that I would tag along and we'd make a short vacation out of it. It would be nice to escape everything for just a little while. At least I'd have something to occupy my mind and help pass the time.

We flew into Boston and the first order of business was to attend a Red Sox baseball game at Fenway Park. The next day we started a sightseeing drive up the coast towards Maine, where Terry would be working. Before heading north, Terry turned the rental car east to go to Cape Cod. After driving around for about an hour, we stopped for lunch at a small, quaint restaurant situated just as we were leaving the cape. During our meal, my beeper went off. This was 1995 and cell phones were not yet a part of our lives. It was a call from my office. I knew that they wouldn't be calling if it wasn't important, so I got up and went to the pay phone that I'd noticed in the small entranceway. My Aunt Faye, who worked at our company, answered.

"Hey, Faye! It's me," I said.

"Hey, Hun! I'm sorry to bother you because I know you're having fun, but I thought you would want to know that the hospital just called for you. They didn't tell me anything and I'd just said that you were out of town, but I'd get you to call them back as soon as I could reach you."

"Okay. Thanks. Do you have the number?"

"Yes, they gave me the direct line for that office. Let me know when you're ready."

I got a notepad and a pen out of my purse. "I'm ready."

She gave me the number. "Call us back after you talk to them and to Terry. Your mom is sitting here with me and we'll be waiting. Hey, I know everything is going to be fine. I just have a feeling. I know you've got to be scared, but it's going to be okay. We love you."

"I love you, too. I'll call you back as soon as I can."

Hanging up, I went and told Terry what was going on. He motioned to the waitress that we'd be right back and followed me to the phone. I dialed the numbers of our long distance calling card, followed by the numbers that would reveal my future. Someone answered, I explained why I was calling and was put on hold. As I stood there, holding the receiver to my ear with one hand and holding onto Terry's hand for dear life with the other, I wondered how long I could actually go without taking a breath. I was pretty sure that it had been awhile since my last.

A lady picked up on the other end. "Mrs. Kasha?"

"Yes, this is Christi Kasha."

"Mrs. Kasha, thanks for waiting. We have the results of your MRI."

"Okay," I mumbled, closing my eyes and squeezing Terry's hand even tighter, a signal for him to somehow magically protect me from the forthcoming news, whatever it happened to be.

The news was simply, "Your test results look good."

Her words confused me. "What do you mean by 'look good'?" I asked.

"Everything was clear. Nothing showed up out of the ordinary on the films."

I still was worried that I might be missing something. "You mean there's nothing wrong?"

The poor lady was probably getting annoyed with me by this time. "You will need to follow up with your doctor, but everything looks okay."

"Oh, thank you," I tearfully spoke into the phone as I smiled at Terry, who by this time had figured out what was going on. "Thank you so much!"

"You're welcome. Enjoy the rest of your trip."

"Oh, I will! Goodbye."

"Goodbye, Mrs. Kasha."

I filled in the blanks for Terry and we replaced holding hands with an enormous hug.

"Well, since you're not dying, I'm going to go finish my lunch. You'd better call your mom." He smiled, gave me a kiss, and walked back inside while I picked up the phone to make one happy call.

So my vision had proven to be true. There was no brain tumor, nor was there any evidence of Multiple Sclerosis. I was relieved and frustrated at the same time. If it wasn't either one of those things, then what was causing the problem? Not to mention that now we were back at square one. I wasn't the only one who was stumped. Dr. Weiner ordered a complete blood workup and a spinal tap. I have been giving blood since I was seventeen years old, so the dozens of vials that were filled with my blood didn't bother me. But as for the spinal tap, I do have some advice: if you ever need to have a lumbar puncture, or spinal tap, done, make sure that the doctor gives the anesthesia time to work effectively before inserting the needle into your spinal column and withdrawing fluid. The pain was excruciating! Yet I had no choice but to endure it. If I moved even the tiniest little bit, it could result in a permanent spinal injury. So I clinched my teeth together and held perfectly still. I kept from moving, but not from crying. Later, I learned that there should be very little pain, if any, during the procedure, and that the doctor probably just didn't wait long enough for the area to become numb. The experience was so horrible that many months later I got upset when I saw the procedure "performed" on a child during a fictional television show. And yet, in some strange way, it reminds me of how life can be: Sometimes the things that shouldn't hurt at all are the very things that cause us the most pain. Often this pain is a result of our sensitivity or is related to the timing in our lives. And it's not unusual for the answers we need the most to be the ones that are the most painful to get.

But when all was said and done, I was glad that I had the test, for it, along with the blood work, ruled out other possibilities, including genetic disorders and cancer. I was extremely thankful, but wished that I had more answers and that I could understand the reasons this had happened to me. In that, I can once again see a reflection of life and the questions that the adversity we encounter often bring.

Dr. Weiner was puzzled. She concluded that her best medical hypothesis was that I had picked up a virus of some sort, one that might have caused someone else to have the sniffles. For some unexplainable reason, it had attacked my optic nerve and had caused some of the cells there to die out, resulting in my blurry spot. Her concern was that it might continue to worsen.

"Christi, we have to try something! At your age, we have to try! I'm going to order some anti-inflammatory steroid treatments. You will have to come to the hospital several days in a row for a series of IV injections. The IV dosage is going to be strong enough that we'll need to wean you off of it by taking the same kind of medicine in oral form for a couple of weeks, with the dosage gradually decreasing."

"Okay," I said, excited that there was something else to try. Maybe I'd actually get off square one.

"Let's give it a shot."

I started the treatments the next week. It wasn't fun, but I was hopeful, and hope can be very powerful in getting us through tough situations. The heavy doses of medicine were rough on me physically, but the other side effects were both shocking and humorous. Well, maybe not humorous to me, but my family members got some comic relief from the situation. Dr. Weiner had warned me about what I might experience while taking the steroids. She said that it could cause mood swings. "No big deal," I thought. "I'm a woman with a menstrual cycle. I can handle that." Come to find out, she meant something a little more extreme. One day at work, I burst into tears because I had to choose a color and a font for some lettering on a sign. Sitting on the floor, my face buried in my arms, sobbing uncontrollably, I finally looked up to see my mom, my brother, and Aunt Faye trying not to laugh at me.

"It's the medicine, Christi. It's the medicine," Mom said soothingly, trying to reassure me that the world wouldn't actually come to an end, no matter which color or font was used. I jumped up, furious for no reason, and stormed out, slamming the door behind me. It was only a half hour before I was laughing so hard over something, or more likely over nothing, that I was practically crying again. "Mood swings?" How about "roller coaster rides"? At least I was able to hold it together enough to not run off any customers, and that's saying something!

During the two weeks that I was taking the oral

medication, one of my accounts was scheduled to have a sign installed in Florida. Terry would be helping my stepdad put it up over the weekend, so he and I drove down in our car, following Mom and Bill in the company truck. The installation complete, we went our separate ways going home, as my parents wanted to make a few stops along the way. We made a stop or two of our own and at one of them I got the chance to learn a couple of things. One was that the mood swings weren't the only side effect that was more extreme than I had anticipated and the other was that laughter can heal and it can show us that even during the storms, we can still feel happiness.

I had been warned that the steroids could also cause an "increase in appetite." From the beginning, I'd decided that if it happened, I was going to go with it! An excuse to eat whatever and as much as I wanted sounded pretty good to me. If it caused me to put on a few extra pounds, well, it was for my health. So that Sunday evening, as we drove home, I told Terry that I was starving. We stopped at a Wendy's restaurant and I ordered the all-you-can-eat salad bar that many of their locations used to have. Terry finished his hamburger and fries and sat waiting patiently for me to finish round three from the bar. When I once again restocked my plate, he mentioned something about needing to fill up the car with gas before getting back on the Interstate.

"Where do you want to go to get it?" I asked, while enjoying a mouth full of pasta.

"I figured that I'd just go right over there." He

pointed out the window to the gas station next door.

I had an idea. "Why don't you go ahead and go fill up while I finish eating."

"No, we're fine. I don't want to leave you here."

"Okay, but I really don't mind." I was more concerned with what I hadn't yet gotten from the bar. Finishing what was on my plate, I told Terry that I was going for more and then for dessert.

"Dessert?" He put a hand to his stomach as if he were feeling nauseous. My return to the table with several different items was the deciding factor. "Maybe I will go ahead and get gas, just to save some time. Are you sure you don't mind?"

"No, not at all. Go ahead, I'll be right here."

"Or in the bathroom," Terry chuckled. "I'll be right back."

"No hurry! I'm good!" I called after him.

I watched out the window and could see him as he filled up the car and then went inside the store to pay. When I saw him heading back to get me, I thought, "Oh, gosh! I'd better hurry!"

Terry walked into the restaurant. "You think you might be ready? They need to restock the bar now," he chided.

"Ha, ha, very funny. Yes, I'm ready. Here, will you carry this bowl of pudding out to the car for me?"

"Bowl of pudding?" He was looking at me as if I were an alien.

"Yes, my hands are full. I've got the ice cream, the cookies, and my Coke. Let's go." It was a delicious trip home. Hey, when life gives you lemons, make lemonade.

With the exception of a few light-hearted moments, the last couple of weeks had been rough, not just from the side effects, but the drugs were physically hard on my body. Finally by the end of the next week, I was finished with all of it and returned to Dr. Weiner's for a follow-up appointment. I wasn't looking forward to it because I hadn't noticed any difference in my eyesight, but emotionally I was prepared for the pending disappointment. I walked through the door to the office devastated, but trying to keep a smile on my face to assure Dr. Weiner that I would be okay. "It didn't work. I can't tell any difference," I announced in defeat to the doctor as she walked me back to the exam room.

"Okay. Let's just see what's going on." I sat down in the chair and she flipped on the specially made electronic eye chart. "Tell me what you can read."

"Well, there's an "E" facing backwards."

"And, now?"

I thought nothing about it as I said. "That's an "E" lying on its back."

"Okay. Try this." The letters were getting smaller and I strained some.

"I think it's an "E" in the normal position.'

"What about now?"

I squinted hard and leaned forward ever so slightly. "I can tell something's there, but I can't make it out."

"All right. That's good for now." Dr. Weiner turned the machine off and the lights in the room on. "Christi," she stood in front of me with a smile on her face, "you just read down to the 20/200 line. Before you were worse than 20/800. That is quite a significant improvement!"

I sat there in stunned silence, then my eyes began to glisten.

"Let me go get Terry and your mom," she said excitedly, and left for the waiting area.

"Her eyesight has improved! Come see!" she proclaimed.

Terry and Mom had a footrace back to the exam room. I embraced Terry with our tears meeting as they rolled down our touching cheeks. Then I hugged Mom, who would later tell me that those few moments were some of the most special of her whole life.

Dr. Weiner interrupted the celebration with "Let's try another round of the steroids. But don't get your hopes up too much," she cautioned.

"Okay, I won't," I lied.

Once we were in the car, Terry told me that as we were walking to the front desk, Dr. Weiner had said, while shaking her head in disbelief, "I never thought it would work. I only tried it because there was nothing left to try." I will always believe that a miracle had just taken place. How often do we miss the miracles that are happening to us because we don't see an obvious difference in our lives right away? How often do we need evidence or someone else pointing it out to us before we can recognize how much better our situation really is or how much closer we are to getting what we want? And sometimes, even when we do see the miracle that has occurred, it can quickly lose its luster under the dark clouds. We take our focus off of what we have been given and direct our attention to what we still don't have, not realizing that the miracle might not yet be complete.

The next round of treatments overlapped with another planned trip. Terry and I were driving out to Nebraska, where Terry and his family are originally from. We were going for the large celebration that was planned for his grandparents' sixtieth wedding anniversary, insted we ended up attending Grandma's funeral. She unexpectedly passed away the day after their anniversary. It was a sweet, sad, beautiful, and sometimes fun trip, not necessarily the easiest combination for someone dealing with mood swings. Although they weren't as severe this time, there were still plenty of opportunities for us to find more ways to cope through laughter.

One day we were in Lincoln, NE with Darren, one of Terry's cousins. As we walked down the sidewalk, I somehow ended up on the outside, right next to the street. I was paying close attention to something Darren was saying and was looking at him as we walked. I turned around to face forward just in time to see the green, metal signpost directly in front of me. I didn't have time to stop and I walked straight into it. The cut on my forehead was minor and other than the bright pink flush of embarrassment covering my face, I was fine, which made me an easy target. Darren and Terry were in stitches and Terry's comment to me was, "I'm so sorry, I thought you could see the big stuff." Yes, even storms can bring humor and laughter into our lives, especially when we can laugh at ourselves. I figured that I might as well make fun of myself. My family certainly wasn't going to miss an opportunity to do so and I didn't want to miss out on the fun.

I'm glad that I had the chance to laugh, escape, and even be emotional over things other than my own situation because dark clouds were once again gathering overhead. I should have heeded Dr. Weiner's warning and not gotten my hopes up, but how could I have not done so? I didn't even worry whether I could tell if there was any change and I was getting used to waiting for results. Shortly after we got back, I went in for my follow-up appointment. What the results that I had been waiting for revealed was that this round of steroids had caused a barely measurable amount of improvement.

"This might mean that they have helped all that they are able to, but let's try one more round to make sure," Dr. Weiner said. So once more I went through the whole process, this time staying at home, resting as much as I could and taking it very easy to give my body the best possible chance to heal. It didn't make a difference. There was no change. I asked Dr. Weiner if we could please try one more round, just to see. She denied my request, explaining that she wanted me to get better, but the long-term risks associated with extended use of that drug could cause me to end up in a wheelchair permanently. "I know how much you want to get better and how important it seems right now, but I'd rather you have the vision that you have than not be able to hold your child one day."

Intellectually, I understood what she was saying and really even agreed with her. The problem was that I had discovered how good hope feels and I wasn't eager to let that go. And it's hard to gauge what's off in the distance when you are focusing all of your energy on the storm at hand. So when asking didn't work, I tried begging. The answer was a compassionate, "No. It's just not worth the risk when it probably won't help. But if you notice anything getting worse, we'll know right away what to do." I admit that I considered faking it.

It seemed that 20/200 was going to be my magic number. In layman's terms what this means is that what you should be able to see at two hundred feet away, I could not see until I was twenty feet from it. My heart ached to know, "Why, why, why?" This time there was no answer, no elevator doors with words spoken in the light. As I realized that there wasn't a rescue boat coming, a wave of depression came crashing in on me. Having been given hope only to have it yanked out from under me was even more heart-wrenching than not having any hope at all. Yes, my eyesight had improved, but not to the extent that it would make much of a difference in my day-to-day activities. I still would not be able to drive, reading things would remain a challenge, and the blurry spot was still there. I felt as though God was messing with me. Why in the name of

Heaven would He arrange for things to happen to improve my sight some, but not enough to make any real difference? And now there was nothing left to try. I just could not get my head, or my heart for that matter, around it. What I couldn't see at the time - no pun intended- was that there are times in life when no rescue boat is going to come, but those are the times that force us to learn how to save ourselves. And then there are other times when what will rescue us is just over the horizon.

However, having just been told that now there was nothing that could save me from what I was going through, I was in no condition to save anyone, especially myself, and I didn't have the strength to swim towards the horizon. My life had drastically changed as I was forced to give up so many of the things that I loved: driving, reading, working, being independent. All along I knew how blessed I was to have Terry, my mom, and other family members who were so willing to help me out in any way that I needed, but while I loved the excuse to spend more time with them, I couldn't fool myself into thinking that it would ever be the same. It couldn't make up for what I had lost. Gaining one thing doesn't necessarily replace losing something else.

Having Terry out of town the majority of the time, working in sales, and not having kids yet had made my schedule extremely flexible. If I wanted to go grocery shopping at ten o'clock at night or run into the drugstore at three o'clock in the afternoon, I just went. Now that lifestyle wasn't possible. A trip to the grocery store was no longer an errand. It had to be a planned event for the weekend while Terry was home. I couldn't just hop in the car and run through a nearby drive-thru if nothing in the refrigerator sounded good. This storm had been scary, but it was the changes that it caused in the currents of my life that were affecting me the most. Many times in the years that have followed, I've noticed how true this often is, for myself and for others. It's the disruption to our lives and the uncertainty of how we will handle the changes that can be more frightening than the adversity itself.

7

The Restorations and Realizations

Life at any time can become difficult, life at any time can become easy. It all depends upon how one adjusts oneself to life.
- Morarji Desai

When Terry was out of town, it wasn't unusual for me to spend the night at my grandmother's house, and it was there that another miracle took place. Late one night, I was talking to Terry on the phone. My grandmother had already gone to bed and I was sitting alone on the sofa in her family room. The television was on, but I wasn't really watching it. At some point during our conversation, something must have been said that struck a nerve and everything just hit me full force. I started crying uncontrollably, in fact wailing would more accurately describe it. Nothing Terry said was doing any good to console me. After I had calmed down some and promised him that I would be okay, we said our "Thank you for today"s, "I love you"s, and "Good night"s and hung up. With my mind focusing on everything and nothing, I turned the TV and the lights off and walked slowly upstairs to the bedroom that I used. I picked up the latest Max Lucado book that I was in the middle of reading. The text was pretty easy to read with the aid of my magnifying glass and his books usually gave me an emotional boost, which I sure did need right then.

But that night I found myself straining more than normal to make out the words. It was probably due to being so tired and upset, but it caused my spirits to sink even lower. That was enough reason for the floodgates to open again. I should have known that if Terry couldn't help, Mr. Lucado didn't stand much of a chance.

Collapsing into a ball on the floor beside the bed, I realized just how miserable I really was. I thought about how lately I was spending more time crying than smiling. I was throwing my life away and I knew it! Something had to change, but I had no idea how to make that happen. So, once more, I did what we have a tendency to do when all else fails. I prayed. "Please, God, help me! I can't do this anymore! You have to do something, please! I don't want to waste one more day of my life feeling this way. Please, God, please do something!" I begged. Not having any other options, I climbed into the bed and quietly cried myself to sleep.

Exactly what happened overnight, I'll never know, but God had once again heard my prayer and answered it. And a miracle took place. My rescue boat had finally come in from over the horizon. I wonder what would have happened if I had only sent up my signal flare sooner.

Did God heal my eyes? No. Instead He did something even more powerful, spectacular, and precious. He healed my heart.

I woke up the next morning feeling like a new person. I was excited to see the sun and thrilled to be alive! I was happy and I was at peace. My eyesight still classified me as "legally blind," but that would no longer stop me from seeing the beauty all around me. I might not be able to read the license plate on the car in front of me or look up numbers in a phone book, but I could see the flowers blooming around my mailbox, the sun setting as I looked out my kitchen window, the clouds floating by in their mysterious shapes, the smile on a child's face, my husband holding up the "I love you" sign in sign language, and the faces of the people I cherished, so who cared about license plates and phone numbers? I saw that I really had very little to be upset over. Yes, life would be different, but I had to decide if different meant worse or better. It wasn't a hard decision.

Just like a rainbow whose beauty and magic aren't visible without the rain's presence, this storm was giving me the chance to see one of the most beautiful things that we can ever witness. I got to see love in action. It had been surrounding me all along, but until that night, I had been so focused on the dark clouds overhead that I didn't really notice it. Suddenly I saw it everywhere!

When Mom would drive nearly an hour to get me out of the house and take me to lunch, there it was. I found it as friends, who were always going "right by my house," would call to say that they could easily give me a ride to and from a get-together. Sometimes love would give me a quick wink when complete strangers seemed more than happy to help out by reading something for me at a store. And it would stare me in the face through the day-to-day actions of my husband. Each time he would read a menu to me, run an errand with me, point out someone that was too far away for me to recognize, or automatically read out loud something that I placed in his hand, I saw love. Perhaps love in action was never more obvious than when Terry and I sat down to eat dinner together. Every single time, he would say a blessing and at some point during it, he would ask God to heal my eyes.

One night, as he finished praying, I said, "Terry, hang on a minute. I feel really bad. You pray for me to be healed every day. You don't have to do that. I mean, my gosh, I don't even ask God to heal me that much!"

He smiled across the table at me, his face radiating love, and simply said, "That's okay. That's my job."

My vision might not have been clear, but I had just discovered the beauty of a committed heart. And, over and over again, I got to see the amazing power and magic that love holds.

The storm had passed, but the sky remained cloudy and waters were still quite choppy.

Paddling could be emotionally exhausting at times and I had to quickly learn that happiness is not a factor of our environments, but a setting of our minds. Now that I could see how blessed I was, I put my pre-set buttons on joy and appreciation, and kept them there as much as possible.

It's a good thing I did because it was a challenging, frustrating, and often embarrassing time in my life. The love and support that I had from my family and friends gave me the strength I needed to keep going with my head up, but it was more than just an adjustment, it was hard.

Because the type of vision problem that I had was so unusual, it was difficult for people to understand. Sometimes it's easier to show compassion when trouble is obvious, but when a problem can't be clearly defined, most of us have less sympathy and patience. I wasn't using a cane or a seeing-eye dog and I would look at whomever was talking to me, so how could I be disabled? In fact, one of my favorite examples of how people would, or perhaps I should say wouldn't, think is that when I would tell someone about my disability, quite often they'd innocently ask, "Well, why don't you just get some glasses or wear contacts?"

I've wanted so badly to respond, "Oh, my gosh! You know, I never thought of that! Thank you! I'm going to call the doctor first thing tomorrow!" Instead, I figured out to include at the beginning of any explanation, "...and it's the kind of problem that glasses and contacts can't fix." It was an easy solution to that issue, but others haven't been as simple to handle.

Some of the hard moments were products of my own insecurities. Many times, as I have asked for help with things like the wall-posted menus at restaurants or the prices on the back wall at a ticket booth, I have wondered if people might think that I was illiterate and that I was trying to cover it up by blaming it on a vision problem. But what could I say? Over time what I have realized is that most people are too busy worrying about their own storms or absorbed in their own thoughts to put that much effort into thinking about what is going on with me or the other people around them. But when something is a big deal to us, we tend to assume that it is of concern to others as well. The truth be told, if someone did notice my struggles enough to give it a thought, the odds are that it didn't rank important enough to warrant a second one.

Perhaps that lack of concern or interest in our fellow man is the root cause for other painful moments. The surprising insensitivities of some people have astounded me. I have had cashiers be completely rude when I asked them to tell me the total, explaining simply that I couldn't see the display on the register.

"It's right there!" one grocery store cashier huffed at me while pointing to the monitor, as if that took less effort than just reading off the total.

"I know, but I have a vision problem and I can't read it from here," I tried to explain.

"Here." she said abruptly, pushing the mounted monitor towards me at a different angle.

"It's too small. I'm still going to have a hard time seeing it." I was beginning to feel for the person in line behind me. With the cashier's next huff, I decided to try another route. "Would you please ask the manager to come read it to me?" That changed her mind and I was shortly thereafter writing the correct amount on my check. Yes, I verified the amount on the receipt with my magnifying glass before I left to make sure that I hadn't paid a "reading service charge." I have figured out since that simply saying, "Oh, no! I don't have my glasses. Would you mind telling me the total?" usually works. That makes it a problem that people can understand and compassion comes more easily.

More than once I've had office staff act bothered that it took me a little longer to sign in at reception desks, even when I mentioned "eye problems." Once at a doctor's office, of all places, I was by myself and was unexpectedly asked to update my records. It was difficult to fill out most of the form, but impossible for me to read and copy the policy number off of my insurance card. After completing everything else, I took the form and my insurance card up to the window and explained the problem. "Would you please write that number down for me?" I asked the lady.

"No, I'm not going to do that. I don't want to be responsible if I copy it down wrong," she informed me.

"So, what would you like for me to do?" I asked, stunned, embarrassed, and angry. The problem was solved when a sweet nurse said she'd be glad to do it for me. I was so grateful.

I wish the people who are willing to get involved and to show love and compassion, even to a complete stranger, could understand just what a ray of light they can be to someone who is fighting the darkness of a physical, mental, or emotional storm. And I wish that the people who act aggravated, who refuse to help, and who don't even attempt the "love your neighbor" concept had any idea of how much I longed to fill out those forms all by myself, read the cash register display, or just be able to sign in without having to work so hard to figure out what each column was for, all while wondering what people were thinking about me. I got good at managing the pain of this adversity, but I never did learn how to not feel it.

8

The Arrivals

> Faith is believing what you can not see...
> the reward of that faith is that
> you will see what you believed.
> - Saint Augustine of Hippo

Even though there were often rough waves and paddling through them could be extremely humbling, life was good. No, life was more than good, it was sweet, fun, and filled with love and magical moments. I found myself coping with the changes and learning to see the glass as half full. I got to be a stay-at-home wife and watch as many episodes of one of my all-time favorite television shows, Little House on the Prairie, as I wanted. At that time it was airing several times a day. Maybe it wasn't a coincidence that the show focuses on a family dealing with life's struggles over and over again in positive ways and the joy they find through their situations. I also got to take leisurely walks with neighbors or by myself. If I wanted to, I could walk a mile to a convenience store or two miles to Kroger. I could stay up as late as I wanted and sleep in until I was ready to get up.

The only problem was when Terry got back from a week of working out-of-town, he was ready to be at home, while I was anxious to get out of the house. We unspokingly and unofficially compromised with one night of going out, usually to dinner and a movie, and the next night, it was pizza and a rented movie at home. We would start off sitting on a blanket on the floor, our legs under the pizza-ladened coffee table that we had pushed up until it was about eight feet from the TV. That way we were close enough for me to be able to really see the picture. But often, by the end of the movie, after I had had enough time to familiarize myself with the characters, we would end up curled up together on the sofa. Oh, yes, life was precious and full of joy! It could be frustrating, but it was a wonderful time that I now look back on fondly, especially on hectic days. What I didn't know then was those special, happy moments that we were sharing would be the strong building blocks for our future.

To make life even better, six months after I quit driving, we got a puppy. Okay, I got a puppy and Terry didn't put up too much of a fight. My brother's dog, a black lab mix, had a litter of eight. He had just moved into a college apartment, so I offered to babysit the litter and then, when they were old enough, I helped him find homes for them. Secretly I had set my heart on one from the get-go. She was black with a little bit of white on her chest and paws, full of life, loved to be held, and I was in love with her little face. When no one chose her, thanks to my redirecting the attention of any admirer to how adorable her brothers and sisters were and pointing out how rambunctious she was, I had no choice but to keep her. She was, after all, kind of my responsibility. One night while talking to Terry on the phone, I calmly and gently made a request. "Now, Sweetheart, tell me again why you don't want a dog right now."

I heard the "Uh, oh, here we go again" sigh, followed by a serious and very rational sounding answer. "Well, the main reason is because we don't have a fence yet."

"But the vet said that doesn't really matter," I reassured him.

"What vet?"

"The one I took her to today."

"What are we naming the dog, Christi?" This time the sigh resounded with defeat. I could just imagine the eyes rolling and the head shaking back and forth.

Together we chose the name Casey, but in retrospect, Lassie would have been more appropriate. That dog saved my life in many ways. I now had something to occupy my time and to focus my energy on. It's hard to feel sorry for yourself when a puppy is licking your face and it's more difficult to be sad at night when a little black ball is curled up in the bed next to you. She was an excuse to get out of the house and go for walks. As far as she was concerned, why would anyone want to be cooped up in a dumb old car when there were so many things to smell along the sidewalk? Casey gave me more reasons to play, to laugh, and to love.

Fifteen years later, she is still part of our family, although she doesn't play anymore. That part of her journey is over. Casey now spends most of her time lying near me by my desk, where I can see her and be reminded that happiness can come to us in unexpected ways, that help can be found in many forms, and that love contains just as much power when it is being given as when it is being received. She won't be with us much longer, so most nights as I head to bed, I'll stop, lean over to pat her head, rub the patch of white on her chest, and whisper a heartfelt, "Thank you, Casey. I love you."

Most of the time the sun was shining on my life and it appeared that the storm had passed, except for the one dark cloud that continued to linger overhead and kept the sun from warming me completely. The one issue that I could not make peace with was the thought that one day when I became a mother, I wouldn't be able to drive my children around. For my whole life, the one thing I had wanted more than anything else was just to be a mom. I think that I was born that way, my baby dolls were real, my younger brothers I considered mine, and I would have babysat for the fun of it, the money was just a bonus. I looked forward to all of the "mom stuff" that went along with that job title. I longed to be the shuttle service to the after-school activities. In fact, the main reason that I was eager to get my driver's license when I was sixteen was so that I could run my brothers around. I craved the trips to the grocery store with little ones in tow and the thought of carpool lines made me smile. Those dreams seemed to have little hope of coming true, so once again, when there was nothing else to do, I prayed.

"God, please. I just want to be able to drive again. That's all I want- just to be able to drive. If my vision is never better than that, if I can never read small print again, that's okay. But, please, God, please just let me see well enough to drive." Over and over again, this prayer was repeated, day in and day out, but the dark cloud stayed where it was and I paddled on.

A couple of years later, Terry decided to leave the company he was working for to manage a new division of his brother's company. The work sounded like something that he would really enjoy, but the best part was that he would no longer be traveling. People assumed that Terry wanted to get off the road to "take care of me" and to be around to help me manage if we had children. I didn't find this sweet, I found it annoying and insulting. I had been doing a pretty good job of taking care of myself for the past three and a half years. And as far as being able to manage with children, my vision wouldn't prevent me from being able to care for them. Some things might be more of a challenge, but not impossible. Be it my eyesight or anything else, I have never made decisions based upon what is the easiest. To me, life is supposed to be about what you enjoy and what will make you the happiest in the long run. Often happiness requires effort.

But most people make assumptions and draw conclusions from their own perception of a situation. We tend to think that everyone will feel and act as we would if we were in their place, and most of the time we do this innocently. It takes a lot of awareness to make ourselves stop and think, "Wait, maybe I should ask about this. That might not be how he's feeling at all." I was shocked and horrified the day a fairly close family member, who was trying to be encouraging, told me that he had met a woman who had only ten percent of her sight but still had children. "So you don't need to feel like you can't have a family. If she could do it, you could too."

"What?" I thought, stunned. I had no idea what to say and I don't remember how I managed to respond. It had never occurred to me that Terry and I wouldn't have children. We had thought ahead of what would make being a stay-at-home mom the most fun for me, like possibly moving to another subdivision which was within easy walking distance of major stores, restaurants, and doctors' offices. But we decided that we were too happy where we were to make that change.

I should have learned right then and there to give people more information concerning the specifics of my problem, but I have been a slow learner in that area. Not focusing on the dark clouds myself, I didn't keep them in the forefront of my mind where I would think to talk about them. I also felt that giving people more information would cause them to jump to more conclusions, and then I would have to counter them as well. I have since learned that living with something twenty-four/seven can sometimes make it less of a disability to you than it seems to someone observing you. Still, I was horrified that a family member didn't understand enough to not compare my disability to that of the heroic woman who had lost ninety percent of her sight. My blurry spot took up maybe three percent of mine. Yes, finding a balance between too much information and not enough information, between what I don't want to dwell on and what I need to try to share has been one of the most challenging parts of my storms. When communication fails, whoever's fault it may be, I just figure that I'll demonstrate my take on life through my actions.

A couple of months after our fifth wedding anniversary, Terry and I were both sitting on the edge of the bathtub one evening, holding hands, and watching the clock, waiting to see if our suspicions were true. We looked liked we were filming a television commercial. At the end of the very long three and a half minutes, the half being because we waited a little extra time just to be sure, Terry smiled at me and said, "Here we go." We stood up, walked to the counter, and looked at the pregnancy test together. It was positive! We were pregnant and I was going to be a mom! If I hadn't seen the beauty and the magic of life before, there was no way that I could deny it now! It's amazing how something so tiny can put all of the big things in perspective!

I absolutely loved every moment of being pregnant. Luckily, I had very little morning sickness, probably because I could sleep through it. See, good can come from any situation. We made a big deal about telling family and friends. I enjoyed the movements, the doctor's visits, decorating the nursery, shopping for clothes and supplies, and even watching my belly grow and grow and grow. It was so wonderful to have something to celebrate! It had been too long.

Those nine months were filled to the brim with happiness, fun, and magical moments! The only thing was that being pregnant had raised my prayer to be able to drive again to a feverish pitch. I'd be okay if I couldn't. But that didn't quench my desire. I was in need of another miracle.

It's been said that God works in strange and mysterious ways. The physical healing that I was waiting for never came, but a phone call did.

Terry's brother, Steve, called out of the blue one day to tell me he had just learned that a good friend of his from high school, Kim, was having some sort of problem with her eyesight. I recognized her name, but had never met her.

"They aren't sure what's wrong, but it sounds kind of like the problem you have," Steve explained. "I'm worried about her and wanted to see if you would be willing to call her. I don't know, I guess I thought it might be nice for her to talk to someone who can relate to what she's going through." The concern in his voice was evident.

"Sure, Steve. I'd be more than happy to call her."

"Okay. Thanks." He gave me her number.

That phone call to Kim led to a new friendship. It turned out that she lived only a couple of miles from me and was pregnant too. I liked her immediately. She was my kind of person and a blast to talk to. A genetic condition ended up being the culprit for the trouble that she was having. Although our problems weren't related and her vision was better than mine, the way it affected our sight was similar enough that we could complain and console each other on the challenges we had. And we were as good as you can get at making fun of ourselves. Yes, Kim was definitely a ray of sunlight that shone through on cloudy days. Although she won't claim it, Kim is also the one who gets the credit for something else. She brought the next miracle to me.

One afternoon she called, excited to tell me that her eye doctor had sent her to the Emory University Low Vision Center to find out more about the optical devices they carry that can help when glasses and contacts can't. I remember that I was sitting at my kitchen table, looking out the window at the trees lining the property of the backyard when she told me that while she was there, they had shown her these special glasses that allowed people with vision problems like ours to be able to drive. I didn't really understand.

"What's your vision measuring?" she asked me.

"20/200 the last time I had it checked," I said.

"That's what I thought!" Kim sounded excited. "You have to have 20/200 or better to qualify for these glasses. I'm going to be tested and try to get them. I thought you might want to check into them too."

"Yeah, I sure do." I couldn't imagine what she was talking about and I wasn't sure that I was actually hearing what I thought that I was hearing. Having learned my lesson from the steroid treatments, I didn't get my hopes up, but I called the number that Kim gave me to make an appointment at the Emory Low Vision Center. I would be seeing Dr. Susan Primo just a couple of days after Kim. Ironically, the office was in the same building that the first neuro-ophthalmologist I had seen was in. It had taken me three years and an awful lot of paddling to go two floors.

I was cautioned that there was more to qualifying for these bi-optics, as they were called, than just 20/200 vision. There would be visual field testing and other intensive tests that would have to be done. "And they are quite expensive," I was warned.

I remember thinking, "How do you put a price tag on a miracle?" as I started thinking about how much room we had on the credit cards and wondering about the equity that we had in our house. Then I calmed down. "First things first. Let's see if I even qualify before I start making financial decisions that might give Terry a heart attack."

Terry and my family were all excited over the possibility of me being able to drive again and were very encouraging and supportive. Friends literally cheered me on. I reminded myself of the odds and was all too aware of how bad it can hurt to have hope yanked out from under me. However, I knew that I would never know if I didn't try, and that sometimes, if you want something badly enough, you just have to tell fear to take a backseat and go for it! So I did.

An immediate reward for the risk I took was Dr. Primo. A sweeter person she couldn't have been. It was so nice to have her positive, upbeat, encouraging attitude when I felt like everything was on the line and one "not good enough" would be the determining factor. The nervousness of having an MRI to look for a brain tumor was nothing compared to this. Finally, after all the testing was done, Dr. Primo had me put on a pair of the bi-optics, which amounted to a sturdy pair of glasses with a black box mounted on top of the frames. The box contained something similar to a binocular lens that you could look through whenever you needed to see off in the distance or needed something magnified to make it clearer. I was told to read the smallest line on the eye chart that I could make out. After I did so, she took the glasses off of my face.

"Well," Dr. Primo began. I held my breath. Then she broke into a smile. "You qualify."

I was in shock. "I... I... do?" I asked, worried that I had heard wrong and that the bubble was about to burst.

"Yes, you do. Your vision meets all of the requirements. You'll have to attend a driving school, which will include actual on-the-road driving time. Then you have to take the road test at a Driver's License office just like you did when you were sixteen. But I'll give you a letter that exempts you from having to take the eye test there. It will probably take a couple of months to get everything done, but after that you can drive again. I will just need to reevaluate you every two years. So, should we order you your own pair of glasses?"

I had gotten my miracle! Sitting in the car crying like a baby, my angel's messages, "All things work together for good for those who love Him." and "This too will pass," came back to me, and faith took on a deeper meaning. I thought back to all of the "why"s that I had asked when my vision didn't improve past 20/200. Looking out the window, I realized that I had just found the answer. God didn't give me what I wanted, He gave me what I needed. My rescue boat had taken a different route than I was expecting.

My miracle didn't come as a complete physical healing. Instead, it came in the form of a friendship and a pair of glasses. The glasses were by no means going to make a fashion statement on the runways of New York, but I thought they were about as beautiful as anything I had ever worn. And my miracle came with a price tag of only two thousand dollars, although I would have happily paid ten times that. But, even better, the priceless lessons that I had just learned on miracles and faith, I got for free.

Then, on August 3, 1997, God outdid Himself! If I thought those bi-optics were miraculous, they paled in comparison to the one miracle that I had been waiting my whole life for. Nothing else in the world mattered the day my daughter, Ansley Elizabeth Kasha, was born! And this eight pound, fourteen ounce miracle, I was able to hold close to my breast. Telling God and Terry, "Thank you for today!" hardly seemed adequate as the day drew to a close. If there were any threatening clouds overhead, I didn't notice them, for I was too busy staring the entire night at the beautiful gift that I held in my arms.

Two months later, Terry was standing a few feet away, holding Ansley who was wrapped up in a soft pink baby blanket, as the state patrol officer handed me my newly printed driver's license. The officer looked a little confused, but smiled sweetly at my tears of joy. Taking a step to the side, I waited while she handed the next person in line hers. It was Kim. For perhaps the first time in history, there were two women together, neither of them complaining about their driver's license picture. We embraced and said we'd call to make plans to meet for lunch the next week. Then we headed home to celebrate with our families.

On the way home, Terry pulled into a gas station to fill up the tank. "I have a feeling that you'll be going through some gas in the next couple of days. I want you to go have fun. Just be careful! Not everyone out there knows to be on the lookout for blind drivers."

Back at the house, I was immediately on the phone, sharing my good news with my family and some friends. There was a lot of squealing going on! And I was moved by how happy everyone was for me. A couple hours later, a friend's husband called. He and I loved to banter back and forth, so I should have seen what was coming, but my head was in the clouds.

"Christi, it's Steve. I just heard the good news

and wanted to call and tell you how happy I am for you! That's awesome!"

"Thanks, Steve! I still can't believe it."

"Listen, will you do me a favor? Will you please fax over your schedule for this next week? I live close to you and I just want to know when I should stay home and when it's safe for me to be out on the roads." I hung up on him with a smile.

The next morning, I buckled Ansley into her car seat to go run errands. I'm not sure that I really needed anything, but you better believe that I was going. As I did, I realized that my miracle had come not at the time that I had asked for it, but when it would mean the most to me.

This afternoon I will drop my second daughter off at gymnastics before taking Ansley to her dance lessons. Yes, God, thank you for today and for the answers to my prayers, even though I haven't always recognized them at the time they arrived.

9

The Second Storm

"Looking for faith is where you will find it."
- Rev. Guy Kent, Questing Parson

    Although it was far from glamorous, I was living the life that I had always wanted. My precious little girl was beautiful, healthy, and happy, and I delighted in being a mom. Because I had regained something priceless to me, I found true joy in taking Ansley places. A trip to the grocery store was a privilege. I had to fight against preaching to harassed moms with screaming, fussy kids to enjoy every second of it because it was a gift. A perfect day started off with going to story time at the library, followed by a shared bowl of sizzling rice soup and some egg rolls at the nearby Chinese restaurant. From there it was on to the soccer fields where Ansley and I would run up and down the field, laughing and practicing our dribbling and passing skills. After nap time in the afternoon, we would cuddle together and watch a kid's video while waiting for

Daddy to get home. By no means were we wealthy, but we had everything that we needed and the house was filled with laughter and love.

Terry and I had both found a way to contribute something meaningful at and through our church, Mountain View United Methodist. Terry was playing guitar with the church's praise music band, which eventually put him in the role of leading not just the band, but also the entire worship service. Hardly a week went by without some member of the congregation expressing to me just how much they had been touched by something Terry had said or done. Talk about a proud wife!

Following my heart's calling, I was a volunteer in the church's children's programs. I have often said that the benefit of leading kids' classes is that you learn more from them than you could ever teach to them. After helping out in that department for many years and getting my heart stolen over and over again by the precious children there, I ended up serving as the Director of Children's Ministries. Kids have always been my passion, so if I was going to have a chance to make a difference, doing so in the life of a child was nothing short of a blessing.

My life was magical! The trouble with my eyes was still a pain in the you-know-what sometimes, but who cared? It wasn't impacting my happiness, and I had almost everything that I could want. There was just one thing that I was missing.

Then in early June of 2000, it arrived. Another television commercial could have been filmed in our bathroom as Terry and I waited to find out if Ansley was going to have a younger sibling. When we went out to eat with grandparents a couple of days later, she wore a t-shirt that read, "I'm a Big Sister" to announce the results.

Finally I was at a point on my journey where I could paddle for the fun of it or I could just lie back and drift. I had no desire or need to change course, life's currents were taking me exactly where I wanted to go. I thought my life couldn't get any better. I was wrong, it could and it would. But first it would have to get worse, much worse.

If someone had told me then that another storm was about to hit, I would have thought they were crazy. "Just look around. There's no evidence of anything threatening. Everything is beautiful, the sky's clear, the breeze is perfect, the water is calm," I would have happily pointed out.

But, just like a tsunami, some of the most devastating waves can't be seen until they reach the surface and are upon us, posing a potential threat like we've never known before. If I had been told how the adversity that I was about to battle would puzzle doctors, break the hearts of my family, and leave me fighting for more than just one life, I don't know that I could have handled it.

Okay, honestly, I would have handled it. Somehow I would have found a way to paddle under the dark clouds that would soon blanket my world. But, looking back, I'm glad there was no crystal ball to show me the whole story. Faith and hope are often the most powerful when we take one step at a time. That step might be making an appointment, walking into a doctor's office, making a tough decision, or just getting through the day, but for that moment that is all we need to worry about. We wouldn't expect to illuminate an entire darkened staircase all at once with a flashlight because there's too much area for it to cover. But by shining the beam directly on the next step or two in front of us, we know that we can reach the top safely. In the same way, worrying about what is too far ahead can spread faith and hope too thin for them to be as effective. We won't have the feeling of security to help us make it through a dark, stormy night. And Terry, Ansley, my family, and I were about to need every ounce of strength and every measure of faith that we could find to get us to the dawn.

August brought with it no indicators that we were enjoying the calm before the storm. After celebrating Ansley's third birthday on a Wednesday, Terry and I left the next day for a weekend convention in Florida. It was not nearly as enjoyable to me as previous ones had been, but I was twelve weeks pregnant and it seemed perfectly normal to feel so tired and for nothing to taste very good. I was just happy to be feeling the evidence of a new life inside of me. Sunday we returned home and spent the next few days catching up from the busy week and getting back into the normal swing of things. I had no way of knowing that in just a few days "normal" would no longer be a part of our lives.

Wednesday evening, as I was taking a shower,

the storm hit. All of a sudden and completely out of the blue, I realized that I couldn't move my left arm or hand. They were hanging lifeless by my side. There was no pain, so I quickly finished showering and then hollered for Terry as I got out. He came into the bathroom. "Look, my arm won't move on its own." I held up my left arm with my right hand, then let go. It fell like a dead weight back to its starting position. When we couldn't find anything else even slightly wrong, we figured that I must have done something like pulling a muscle, but without the pain. Terry helped me get dressed and we ended up laughing hysterically as we flopped my pathetic arm around like it was a toy. Being baseball fans, we were familiar with what is referred to as "Tommy John" surgery for arm injuries. So Terry had fun diagnosing me as needing it.

"I'm going to throw a baseball at your head if you don't quit messing with me!" I defended myself.

"Not with that arm you're not."

Eventually we went to bed, exchanging our "Thank you for today"s.

The morning brought more laughter at my expense as I attempted to put on deodorant and get dressed. Terry had to help me with both. Since none of the feeling had returned, I called the doctor. After explaining the situation and my lack of any other symptoms, I was given an appointment time for the following morning. Terry left for his office, only ten minutes away, telling me to call him if something changed or if I needed anything. He said he'd come home to help me with lunch. I seized the chance to sit around just relaxing and hanging out with Ansley. There was some housework that begged to be done, but I used the excuse that I wouldn't want to risk putting any more strain on whatever I had injured. Other than not being able to use one arm, everything went well that day. When Terry got home from work, he said that maybe it would be a good idea if he handled cooking us something for dinner. He did and the three of us, well, three and a half, ate at the kitchen table before he had to leave for praise team practice.

"I'd be more than happy to miss it tonight," he offered.

"No need for you to unless you just want to use me as an excuse. I'll skip Ansley's bath tonight and put her to bed a little early, then I'll watch TV until you get home."

"Okay, but don't attempt undressing or dressing yourself, please. I don't want to miss the entertainment." He dodged my punch, grabbed his guitar, and ran down the steps.

"I hope you break a string!" I hollered at him.

"Ans, help your mommy and be a sweet girl. I'll come kiss you when I get home."

"Okay, Daddy, I will."

"I've got my phone. Call me if you need me, Sunshine. Love you!"

"Love you too! Be careful."

He left and I cleaned up the kitchen with Ansley's "help." It's too bad that kids aren't as eager to help when they are old enough to really do some good as they are when they're little. Then we managed to get her pajamas on, brush little teeth, and take her vitamins. In her room we read a couple of books, rocked, and I sang a couple of her favorite lullabies. It was somewhat tiring trying to do everything one-handed and I was ready for a rest, so I kept it as short as possible. If I had it to over again, I would sing each and every song that she requested.

The next morning there was no change. Mom came over to drive me to the doctor. Other than the pregnancy fatigue, I felt okay and the exam didn't reveal anything out of the ordinary. The doctor told me, "Well, everything with the baby looks good and other than your arm, you seem fine too. I think you have an elbow or shoulder injury, which means that you need to see an orthopedist. I'd be glad to recommend someone or you can look up a provider that is covered by your insurance. But it's the weekend so you might not be able to get in to see anyone until Monday. You should be fine until then. Just take it easy and don't overdo it."

"Actually, we have a friend of the family who is in that field. I'll start by calling him."

"Good idea. Let us know if you need anything," the doctor handed me my checkout papers.

"Will do. Thanks."

Back in the car, I told Mom what the doctor had said and then called Terry. As I expected, he was quite amused that his diagnosis had been confirmed. But my mother saw nothing funny about the situation. The diagnosis didn't make sense to her as we could not begin to imagine how I might have sustained such an injury. "I don't know," she just kept saying, shaking her head. The truth is her maternal instincts had kicked in.

An appointment with our friend was made for Monday morning at ten o'clock, but setting it ended up being a waste of everyone's time. I never made it. Early Sunday morning I woke up feeling really bad and decided to stay in bed. I persuaded Terry to go on to church where he was needed. I told him when Ansley woke up, I'd let her watch TV until he got home. "Tell them I'm sorry. Myrna will get someone to cover my Sunday School class, but would you ask Judi if she will cover Children's Church for me?" I requested.

"Done deal. I'll have my phone on vibrate during the service, so you call me if you need anything and I can leave right then." He kissed me. "Take care of yourself."

Not too long after he left, I was on the phone. "Mom, can you come up here? I don't feel right. I woke up not feeling good, so I stayed home from church, but I told Terry to go on. Now I'm worse. I don't want to call him yet because they just started the service. But I thought someone should know and I might need help with Ansley."

"What do you mean you don't feel right, Christi? I want to know what's going on and if I need to call Terry or an ambulance?"

"No, I'm okay right now. I just feel so sick and well, just weird."

"Are you having trouble breathing or anything?"

"No, nothing like that. I'm just so yucky and weak. It wasn't this bad when Terry left. I'm scared it'll get worse." I was hoping that she couldn't hear the fear in my voice; maybe I just sounded sick. But if I was calling, she would know something wasn't right.

"I'm on the way."

It took her less than an hour to get to my house, but by the time she let herself in, I knew that I was going downhill. "Mom," I said, lying on the sofa, "something's not right. Maybe I should go to the emergency room."

"Should I call 911?"

"No, I don't think that we need to do that. I just want to see a doctor."

"Okay, let's go. What about Terry?"

Looking at my watch, I said, "He should be packing everything up after the service right about now. I'll call him."

"You want me to call him for you?"

Already dialing his cell phone, I pictured his face. "No, I'd better call or it will scare him to death."

He answered and I explained what was going on. "Hold on just a few minutes. I'm going with you. I'll be right there. I'm walking out the door." His voice sounded strong and in control. I felt a wave of relief come over me. I had my mom, now I wanted my husband.

It only took him five minutes to get home, but that was all the time that Mom needed for fear to take hold. After hanging up the phone, I got up to go to the bathroom. She saw immediately what a hard time I was having standing up and how I was barely able to walk. I was stumbling and nearly doubled over and I had to hang onto the wall for balance and support. She knew that there was something very, very wrong, but she tried to hide it because Ansley was now up and in the room with us. Mom had already arranged for my brother and sister-in-law, Scott and Denise, to meet us at the hospital to pick up Ansley. The moment Terry walked in, she gave him a telling look and said simply, "Let's go." He got me into the car for the fifteen minute drive there.

My decision to seek medical attention was definite and clear, but it opened the door to a period in my life that was anything but. My recollections of the events at the hospital that day are varied and sketchy. Some I remember with perfect clarity. Others I have learned about over the years through the accounts of my family members.

I don't remember the drive to the hospital, Scott and Denise arriving, or Ansley leaving with them, but I do remember being in the exam room and the doctor telling me that I needed a CAT scan.

"A CAT scan? Wait! Won't that hurt the baby?" I wanted to know.

"Well, there is some risk, just as there is with any x-ray procedure during pregnancy. But we need to be able to get a picture of your brain to find out what is causing your loss of mobility."

"Is there something else that you can do that isn't so dangerous?" My hand that still worked instinctively covered my belly.

101

"We could do an MRI, but it's more complicated and will take longer and...."

"Okay, let's do that," I interrupted. "I've had them before and they don't bother me. It's safe for the baby?"

"Yes, there's no radiation, so there's no risk to the fetus."

Decision made.

I was taken back for the test. As it turned out, this procedure that I had requested and that I was almost looking forward to, ended up being a nightmare. Unlike the previous MRIs for my vision, this time lying still on my back caused excruciating pain. There were no bright lights or reassuring words this go around, just me counting backwards from sixty once, then twice, then again and again, hoping to gauge the amount of time remaining and giving me something to focus on. This procedure ran a very close second to being as horrific as my spinal tap had been. After what seemed like an eternity, it was announced that we were finished and I was rolled out of the machine. All I could think was, "I survived! I made it!" I was getting more than just results from these tests, I was learning lessons about pain not lasting forever and about how we have inside of us the strength to endure most situations if we have a strong enough reason to do so.

The next memory I have is lying in a hospital room with a doctor talking to us about what was wrong. The MRI had shown that there were lesions on my brain. Based on the look of them and my vision history, it was most likely showing that I did have Multiple Sclerosis. He wasn't sure why the disease had not shown up on the previous MRI's, but it wasn't important at that moment. The diagnosis would be confirmed by a specialist, but it was taking longer than normal because of it being a Sunday. I was in a fog, but the seriousness of having MS, I understood. My thoughts tried to make sense of it all and what it meant for the future- mine, Terry's, Ansley's, and the baby's.

Sometime later, the doctor returned. After looking at the MRI films some more, it had been determined that I might not have MS. Instead, the doctors were now thinking that I had suffered a series of small strokes. The main concern was what had caused them. Initially, all I could do was celebrate the fact that I didn't have this horrible, life-altering disease. But then I began the internal debate over which would be the lesser of two evils: Multiple Sclerosis or having strokes for some unknown reason at thirty-two years old, all while being pregnant? I never did settle on an answer.

Many hours passed before the specialist got back with his diagnosis. He confirmed that it was MS. I was kept overnight for observation and given medication through an IV, the same anti-inflammatory steroids that I had been given for my eyes. Recalling how Dr. Weiner had turned down my request to try one more round to see if it would improve my eyesight any further, the joke now became that I was so stubborn that I'd go to this length just to get more of that drug.

The next afternoon I was released to go home.

The MS episode would just have to run its course and I would simply need time to rest and recover. Once home, Scott and Denise brought Ansley, whom they were still taking care of, home to us. I'm sure that plans were discussed by my family on how to help me out while I was recuperating, but I have only one memory from that day, Monday, August 14, 2000. It is a flash of me having trouble getting ready for bed after taking a shower. I was standing in the bathroom and Terry had to help me put on an old comfortable nightshirt that I loved. After that, the next four days and the storm that consumed our lives, I only know about from the recollections of my family.

Terry helped me to bed, then Mom and Bill kissed me goodbye and left after I was settled in. They had decided to go home since the only thing that either of them could do that night was to get a good night's sleep so they'd be ready to help me the next day. Mom says that she'll never forgive herself for leaving. She remembers how badly she didn't want to go, but naturally thought that she was just being an overly concerned mom. What was she going to do, watch me sleep? So she made herself leave. Maternal instincts are strong.

After they were gone, Terry and Ansley snuggled together beside me in our king-size bed. They watched the Braves baseball game on television while I slept. Suddenly and without any warning, I began having seizures. According to Terry, the ones you see on the medical shows on TV are nothing. He says that I was literally bouncing on the bed. Not knowing what was happening and doing the only thing that he could to protect his little girl, he told Ansley to go to her room and stay there. Both of our hearts now break at the thought of that tiny angel scared and alone.

Terry sprung into action. He called 911 on our house phone and his parents, who lived two miles away, on his cell phone. "Dad, something's wrong with Christi! I've got 911 on the other phone! Please come get Ansley!" he shouted into the receiver. Whether Terry heard his dad's response or not was of little consequence. "Grandpa" had retired from law enforcement and now his son and granddaughter were in distress. He was on the way. Terry, waiting for the paramedics, had to unlock the front door, put Casey in the basement, and then watch what he thought was his wife dying, helpless to do anything as the seizures continued. The paramedics arrived, loaded me up and wheeled me out to the ambulance. At some point, Terry called my parents and told them to head back and meet us at the hospital. I had more seizures in the ambulance and in the ER. They finally got them to stop, and still thinking this was a result of Multiple Sclerosis, put me back on the steroids and admitted me.

Although I don't remember any of it, I was in and out of consciousness. The medicine wasn't working and I was growing weaker and weaker with each passing hour. As the time went by, the paralyzation in my arm and hand spread down to my left leg and eventually affected the whole left side of my body, including my face. When I was awake, I was aware enough to sign my own hospital forms and was getting up to go to the bathroom with someone helping me. But I was getting worse and losing ground quickly. Family members have said they were literally watching me slip away. At some point, my brother, Matt, who was working in Connecticut with the dance company, Pilobolus, was called. "You'd better come home," Mom told him, crying. He left work where they were rehearsing a new piece and flew home immediately.

Terry was at my bedside constantly. Tuesday night he couldn't get me to respond to him the way I had been. I was making strange movements with my face, moaning and groaning, and having, what he believed, were mini-seizures. He kept trying to tell the nurses on duty that something wasn't right, but he couldn't get anyone to check out what he was saying. "It's just her reacting to the medicine," he was told over and over again.

The next morning, Terry talked to the doctor who was in charge of my care and explained what I had been doing overnight. This doctor will always be a hero in my book. He listened, examined me once again, and then had the humbleness to say to Terry, "I have no idea what this is or what's wrong. You need to transfer her somewhere where they can find out and treat her." His honesty and humility saved my life.

Terry credits Scott for the transfer happening. Not having slept much for days, an emotional wreck, and knowing that whatever decision he made could cost me my life, Terry was having a difficult time deciding what to do. When Scott arrived that morning, Terry told him about what happened overnight and what the doctor had said.

"Then we need to get her out of here. Now! Let's transfer her to Piedmont." That's all Terry needed to hear and the paperwork was started.

Sometimes decisions are hard, not because of the "what now"s, but because of the "what if"s. Often we know what the next step should be, but then we notice the possible negative outcomes that our choice might lead to and it can be difficult to act, especially when emotions are running high and something very important is on the line. For my precious husband, this was never more true. He had been told by the doctor that he needed to have me transferred, but at the same time had been warned that doing so could kill me. Scott provided Terry with the reassurance he needed that he was making the best choice. There's a time in every ball game, and in every storm, when you might need to pass the ball off to have the best chance of winning. You can be too covered to judge what your next move should be, while someone else may very well have a better perspective. As it was with Terry and the doctor, sometimes the hero is the one who knows when to let go.

The Mayo Clinic had been considered, but I was most likely too weak to survive the flight there. The doctors and my family had been in contact with my neuro-opthalmologist, Dr. Weiner, for consultation and advice. Moving to Piedmont Hospital was her recommendation. "The best neurologists in Atlanta are here. Say the word and I'll make the arrangements."

The word was said and Piedmont Hospital it was. Still Terry was cautioned that even the direct, short thirty minute ambulance ride there might be more than my body could handle. But apparently even I agreed that there wasn't a better option because I signed my own transfer papers. So look out, Piedmont, here I come!

Our beautiful little girl had been staying with relatives during this time and it had been days since Terry had seen her. With the new hospital being farther away, he wanted to spend some time with just her before I was transferred. Worried about leaving me, but knowing what I would want him to do and that Ansley needed him right then more than I did, he went to pick her up. They headed to the McDonald's that she and I frequented, the one with the cool playground. There they got to laugh and play together. I'm guessing that Ansley wasn't the only one who needed that special time.

While he was gone, the transfer arrangements progressed quickly and they needed to go ahead and move me. Terry finally called an end to his date and forced himself to take Ansley back to her aunt and uncle. He left with both of them in tears.

From there he headed to the new hospital. Merging onto the expressway, he found himself immediately behind an ambulance. My brother, Matt, waved at him from the back window. Yes, it was the ambulance carrying me. The odds of that happening in metro Atlanta on one of the busiest Interstates are beyond amazing. It goes to show that some things can work together for good when we just let them happen because we are taking care of first things first, and some connections really can't be broken. Terry followed me to the hospital and into the worst of the storm.

I was admitted to the Intensive Care Unit. Unconscious and completely unresponsive, it was obvious that I was losing ground. At some point that day, a doctor confirmed for Terry that I had slipped into a coma. When asked just how bad I was, the doctor explained it to my family in terms of "On a scale of one to ten, with ten being the worst, I'd say she's at a nine tonight." My husband doubted that I would live to see the morning. He has since learned not to play the odds when betting on me.

The next day the specialists that had been brought in, including one of the best neurologists, Dr. Douglas Stuart, and a top internal disease doctor, gathered Terry and other family members in a small room to explain that they were fairly certain of what was wrong. In order to confirm their suspicions, I needed a test where dye would be injected into my leg and directed up to my brain, giving a clearer image of the lesions there. It was somewhat invasive and there was a possibility that my body would not be able to tolerate the procedure. The other thing they wanted understood was the sad news that there was no way that the baby I was then thirteen and a half weeks pregnant with could survive this test.

Terry told them, his heart breaking in more ways than one, "Do what you have to do to save my wife." No one in my family disagreed.

I was taken off on a gurney to have the procedure done. My father says that as they wheeled me past where he was standing in the hallway, he prepared himself that it might be the last time he would see his little girl alive.

While the test was being performed, Mom asked Dr. Weiner, who was following up on me, what she thought the chances of survival were.

Dr. Weiner shook her head with a look of compassion as she quietly told Mom, "I'm sorry. There really isn't any hope for the baby."

"No," Mom corrected in a mix of fear and relief, "for Christi. Is there any hope for Christi?"

"Oh, for Christi. Well, I'm not going to lie to you, it's very serious. But don't give up on her yet. She has three things working in her favor, she's young, she's strong, and she's stubborn."

Mom smiled and nodded. "Yes, she is that."

When the test was over, I was still in a coma, but I was alive! By no means was I out of the woods though. The results confirmed what the doctors had thought. I had a rare disease called "viral encephalitis," an inflammation and swelling of the brain caused by a virus. In my case, the virus was the herpes simplex two virus, the same one that causes cold sores and fever blisters. Although most of my immediate family members have experienced those symptoms, I have never had a fever blister in my life and still haven't to this day. While an estimated eighty percent of the population is a carrier, blood work revealed that I had only contracted it within the past several months, possibly because of my immune system being weakened as a result of the pregnancy. In extremely rare cases, the virus finds its way to the brain and causes the encephalitis. The statistics for this disease in the United States are two people out of a million each year. Lucky me! In fact, one of the doctors explained to Mom that in addition to me not exhibiting the normal symptoms of viral encephalitis, the reason the doctors at the other hospital had assumed that this was related to my vision and were so quick to think that it must be Multiple Sclerosis was that the odds of me contracting two viruses that each caused separate and extremely rare neurological problems were astronomical. Well, who wants to be normal anyway? Nothing exciting or special about that.

Treatment was started immediately, but even though the doctors now knew what needed to be done, there were other factors to reckon with and I was in a fight for my life. One main concern was how long it had taken to diagnose my condition. After four days of viral encephalitis going untreated, a patient's chances of survival drop significantly. Also, how conscious the patient is at the time treatment is started can play a major role in the outcome. It had been nine days since I had lost the use of my arm and treatment was started while I was in a coma. My age and pregnancy were working against me as well. The odds definitely were not looking good. Knowing what to treat me for was one thing, saving my life was another.

The medical team cautioned my family, who

were taking turns holding two-persons-at-a-time bedside vigils in the ICU, that even if I lived, I would most likely remain in the coma for weeks and require a hospital stay of several months. After that, we were facing a life that might never be the same again. There was a very strong possibility of brain damage. Less than forty percent of survivors come away with minimal or no long term neurological effects, including tremors, seizures, memory, communication, and behavioral problems. Yes, survival might have been the immediate concern, but by no means did it end there.

Terry has told me of how he would sit by my bed while I was in the coma, his hand cupping my face as he talked to me. Although he was silently making plans for what to do if I didn't live, including the decision to have me buried in the cemetery of the country church I had attended as a child and burying me with my wedding band on, but saving my engagement ring for Ansley, he couldn't bring himself to actually use the word "death." Instead, he would say over and over again to me, "Defeat is not an option. We need you. Don't give up, Sunshine. Fight!" And every night he would continue to tell me, "Thank you for today. I love you!" Besides hoping that I could hear them, the words reminded Terry that at least we were still sharing our days and lives together. I have a feeling that my heart answered back.

10

The Sun and the Rain

*"And in the end
it's not the years in your life that count,
it's the life in your years."*
- Abraham Lincoln

I must have heard Terry's directive. I woke up from the coma two days later. The doctors had predicted weeks, but they weren't figuring into the equation my experience with the power of love. I opened my eyes to see Terry standing at the foot of the bed on one side and my brother, Matt, standing on the other. It is the first memory I have after the one of me trying to put my nightgown on the night I had the seizures.

Terry and Matt happened to be the two who were in the room with me when the doctor came in on his rounds. He pulled my eyelids apart to check my response. Terry said he knew right away that I had regained consciousness because my eyes immediately looked over and focused on him. He ranks that moment as one of the happiest in his life, rivaled only by watching our children being born. For me, that memory is like a clear photograph and will be eternally priceless and treasured. There was no fear on my part and I don't remember being confused. It was as though things were just as they were supposed to be. Two of the people that I loved the most in the world were there next to me, smiling. Everything must be okay.

Terry stayed with me while Matt went to the waiting room to share the news. Mom says she remembers him coming down the hall towards her saying, "Come on, come on!" When she first saw him walking quickly and motioning, her heart sunk and she thought, "Oh, no!" But then she realized that his gait was not one of fear or sadness. As he got closer, she saw his excitement and jumped up to meet him, and they returned to my room.

I was conscious, but so weak that I didn't have the strength to keep my eyelids open. Terry would gently hold them apart for me so that I could see my family as they came in to celebrate. In addition to the weakness, my left side was still immobile. Even if I had been able to do so on my own accord, the feeding tube that had been put down my throat prevented me from speaking. I had wires and tubes running in and out of my body everywhere. But I was alive and awake! Once again, God had done something amazing in my life. This miracle sure didn't look as beautiful as others had, but the realness of the machines, wires, tubes, and tears all pointed to just how miraculous it was!

It still seems strange that there are four days that are lost to me. I was fighting through the worst storm of my life and didn't even know it. I'm not alone. How often have some of us not realized what we were battling until after we came away from it? Maybe it wasn't a battle in the physical sense as mine was at that time, but we may have been fighting through other kinds of storms like those with relationships, depression, addictions, or tough day-to-day circumstances? Whether we end up with positive or negative results, the emotions that go along with having to fight for our lives and for our well-being can be traumatic. I guess in some ways I'm lucky; because I don't remember, I don't have to carry around the emotional battle scars of those four days. I see the effect that week had on my family. Even though I survived, Terry, Ansley, Mom, Dad, Bill, Matt, and Scott all get this pained look on their faces when talking about that period. Perhaps my not being able to remember was caused by my body's natural survival mechanism. We can only handle so much at once and I needed my strength to fight physically. The emotional trauma might have been too much for me. Sometimes during life's storms, when we don't understand something or when we don't have all of the information that we want, we need to remember that there might be a good reason for it. It's possible that someone knows better than we do what we need to focus on in order to survive.

My first attempt to communicate happened

about forty-five minutes after I woke up. It caused a wave of panic to rush through Terry. He and Matt were again both in the room with me, repeatedly reassuring me that I was in the hospital, but that I was okay and that everything was going to be fine. Terry noticed that my right hand was twitching and my fingers were moving. "Matt," he fearfully said, pointing it out, "I think she's starting to have another seizure."

My brother turned to go get the nurse, then hesitated. "No, look! She's trying to sign something!"

I knew a minimal amount of sign language, including the alphabet and had taught it to Terry and Ansley. Matt also knew a good bit and recognized that I was finger spelling. After several minutes and a couple attempts, they were able to decipher the message that I was trying to spell out with my weakened fingers. Terry laughed and breathed a sigh of relief for the first time in almost a week. "She's asking who's covering Children's Church!" He shook his head in amusement. "She's fine! She's going to be okay!"

I didn't understand what was so funny. They had told me it was Friday, which meant a revival had started at our church. I was signed up to teach the kids' classes. If I wasn't going to be there, I needed to make sure that it got covered. Putting a hand on each side of my face, my husband leaned down close to me and looked me in the eyes. "Kay is taking care of it. You don't need to worry. She's got it covered. I promise!" I can still hear his voice assuring me and see his face, smiling so sweetly down at me, his eyes filled with tears. Then he kissed me.

My first attempt at communicating verbally was also to Terry, but for completely different reasons. Like many other things during that period, I don't remember it, but my husband has emotion in his voice each time he recounts the story to me. He says that my words were practically incoherent because of half of my mouth, tongue, and face still being paralyzed. As he was getting ready to leave one night, it was obvious that I was trying to speak. Leaning down close, he heard the mumbled words that perhaps no one else would have understood. It wouldn't have mattered. The words were, after all, meant solely for Terry.

"Aik ou or ou-ay!"

"Thank you for today, Sunshine!" he responded, embracing me. The sun peeked through the clouds.

The events of the next few weeks and their order are scrambled in my memory. Most of the time passed as I slept, but there are some things that stand out in my mind. I think back to my family members and friends who took the time to call or to come see me, often bringing with them thoughtful gifts, smiles, and encouragement.

One day I was surprised by a phone call that I received from an old friend, Tim. He and I had dated for a year in high school, but had remained friends ever since, although it had been quite awhile since we had talked to each other. He heard how bad off I was through prayer requests at his church, where I had been a member for eight years before Terry and I got married.

"Christi, do you know who this is?"

"Tim! Hey!" I know it must have surprised him how slurred my speech was and how much trouble I had talking, but he acted as if he didn't notice.

"I heard about you being sick at church and just wanted you to know that I'm thinking about you and praying for you." I knew that he meant it. "Listen, I want you to know that when I heard that we came close to losing you, a certain Garth Brooks song came to mind." Tim's the one responsible for me being a country music fan, so now he was speaking a shared language.

"If Tomorrow Never Comes?" I guessed. I just knew. The lyrics of the song share a message about wondering "if tomorrow never comes" will someone special know how much you loved him or her. The singer regrets that he didn't share his feelings for loved ones before he lost them. He learned that there might not be a second chance to tell someone how you feel, so he wants to make sure that person knows of his love.

"That's the one," Tim said. "And I mean it in a way that would not be upsetting or disrespectful to your husband. After all, I have tons of admiration for him. He's the one who has lived with you all these years."

"Thanks, Tim. Love you too," I threw back sarcastically.

"Hey, take care of yourself, okay? I need you

around. I've got to have somebody to mess with and to keep me on my toes. Let me know if you need anything. And tell Terry and your family that we are praying for them too."

"I will." It was time to be serious. "Thank you for calling, Tim. It means a lot. And just in case tomorrow never comes, I love you too."

Then there was the day that Tami walked into my room. When I realized who it was, I squealed and moved quicker than I had in a week. She was one of my two best friends from college. I had not seen her in a couple of years. A mutual friend heard through a prayer request at her church that I was in the hospital and had called Tami at work to tell her. It just so happened that Tami was supplementing her teacher's salary by working as a manager at a restaurant next door to the hospital. The story goes that she immediately left work to come over and ended up literally running into Terry as he was walking down the hall. Tami visited often, sometimes with food from her restaurant, but always bringing laughter and love into the room with her to lift my spirits. In the years that followed, she moved and changed jobs, and we lost touch. I tried a few times to track her down, but was never successful at doing so. "Sooner or later, we'll get back in touch," I told myself. I should have followed Tim's example.

A couple of years ago, I was in desperate need of a laugh or two and could have used Tami's friendship. I decided to try again, and this time a little harder, to track her down. "Maybe Tracy knows how to reach her," I thought, wondering why I hadn't tried this route before. Tracy is the mutual friend who let Tami know that I was in the hospital. Facebook was new on the scene and Tami wasn't on it, but Tracy was. Late one night I went to Tracy's page to send her a message. Her status for that day read, "Mourning the death of my good college friend, Tami Smith..." I couldn't believe my eyes. I burst into tears, causing Terry to run downstairs from our bedroom to see what was wrong. What was wrong was that I didn't go the extra mile that she and Tim had. I didn't keep up with my friend so that I could be there during her storm. I didn't let her know how much I loved her. Now I would have to live with the regret that as far as our friendship went, tomorrow would never come. I was going to miss her so much!

Tami had lost a very private battle with bone cancer. Hardly anyone knew. But she left this world the same way that she had lived in it- by making a difference. In life, she had served in the Peace Corps, had chosen to teach in inner city schools, and had taken the time to help a friend get through her storm and make her smile. In death, she donated her body for research and had taught that friend to never assume that we can wait until tomorrow to show our love for someone. Tami, I'm sorry that I never got the chance to be there for you or to let you know the comfort that your mere presence gave me during my darkest hours. God bless you, my friend.

In contrast to my memories of the special visits and phone calls, I also can recall, sometimes too vividly, many of the medical procedures during my hospital stay. There was the frequent changing of the needle's location that was ever-present in my arm and this stupid little hand held monitor that I had to blow into to measure the strength of my lungs. I didn't need it to tell me. The fact that I was barely strong enough to talk answered that. Why is it that recovering can make you feel like you are somehow failing instead of getting better? I didn't mind monitoring my progress, I just didn't want others to see how bad I was and how little improvement there had been. I wanted them to believe that the hope we were all clinging to wasn't futile. The problem was that since I was too weak to hold the box by myself, I had to have help. Wouldn't life be so much prettier if we could hide the messiness of our battles and only display our victories? And asking for help and accepting it when it is offered would be easier and would feel better if it wasn't usually needed at the time when our troubles have caused our self confidence to already be running low. It would be easier, yes, but then other people wouldn't know how hard we have been fighting to get through the adversity and how meaningful each small victory is to us.

However, winning out over the unpleasant medical memories are the ones I have of reaching certain milestones. While they might not seem significant or spectacular, they were celebrated and they gave me hope. Life is a matter of perspective. For me, being allowed to walk down the hall instead of riding in a wheelchair, taking a bath or a shower, and going to the bathroom by myself were all incredibly important. Another one of my favorites is the day that they finally took out that stupid feeding tube. I got to eat! Hospital food never looked so good.

In addition to fighting off the virus and dealing with the sickness, there were some very difficult moments that didn't have anything to do with medical procedures or what I couldn't do. Instead it was about finding out what I was doing wrong. I remember Mom telling me not to talk so loud when someone came to visit. We didn't realize it yet, but my hearing had been affected by the disease and I couldn't tell how loud I was talking. Apparently I was also acting like a little kid who is overly excited, especially when someone came into the room to visit with me. Mom said it was like watching me go through stages of childhood all over again. I'm surprised that she didn't instruct me to use my "indoor voice" and to "sit still like a big girl." The concern was that I couldn't control my emotions or that I didn't understand what behavior was appropriate. Those things would be indicators of some sort of brain damage. I understand why this would be the first thing that would come to the minds of my family. They had been told that brain damage for me was a probability, not a possibility. But that was their concern, not mine.

I can still feel the emotion that I was experiencing at that time and yes, I was extremely happy! I might have been doped up, in and out of consciousness, and still very sick, but I was aware enough to understand that I had been given another chance at life. I might not have been able to move much or speak without the words sounding slurred and garbled, but I could love. And love I did! Every person that came into that room was a gift to me, perhaps because lying in a hospital bed hour after hour, day in and day out, has a way of making ordinary things seem extraordinary, or perhaps life had just taken on a new kind of beauty and happiness. This journey might be tough, but I was determined to see and appreciate the joy in it.

If I wanted joy, there was one visitor that brought more of it into my room than all of my other visitors combined. And no one said a thing about how excited I acted this time. Five days after I woke up from the coma, the most beautiful little blond-haired, blue-eyed girl that I had ever laid eyes on was carried into my room. In my memory, there was only her and me. "Mommy!" Ansley squealed as she was handed to me. With my right arm, I pulled her to me and held onto her for dear life. She snuggled her precious little face into my neck, both of us crying. It had been nine days since we had been together, the last time was as the seizures started.

With her little hands, she started rubbing my neck. Rubbing her own neck or the neck of whoever was holding her was her own little way of comforting herself, her unique version of Linus' blanket. The neurological damage caused by the virus had left my nerves raw, feeling as if they were on fire, especially when contact was made with my skin. The rubbing motion Ansley was making was torturous and I was weak from holding her, and yet my baby could have kept it up for as long as she wanted. This was the moment for which I had defied the odds. This was why I had lived! This was love!

Somewhere during that time, Terry and I were told that another miracle had taken place, one that left the medical staff in shock. Our baby was alive! Despite the odds, going against all of the medical predictions, there was a strong heartbeat. I will always believe that I had fought to live not for my own life, but for the lives of my two children, one who was waiting for me, the other whom I would have to wait for.

This miraculous, precious news, however, did not arrive without bringing complications with it, complications that would bring turmoil to our hearts and new meaning to the word patience. Yes, the baby was alive, the doctors told us, but we needed to be fully aware of what we were dealing with. It was not a matter of whether the fetus had sustained brain damage, but of how severe the brain damage would be. Tests could be run to gain some information, but there might not be any way to determine the type or the extent of the problem. So the first question posed to us was did we even want the tests performed. The answer was an easy, "Yes." Then we were given a date of about six weeks down the road. It was the last day that we could choose to end the pregnancy if we decided that is what we should do.

I was horrified! This baby's life that I had tried so hard to protect was now in my hands. I found myself having to look at choices that, under most other circumstances, I wouldn't even be considering. For me personally, and without judgement of others, abortion would have never been an option in the event of an unplanned pregnancy, even as a teenager. I wouldn't have ever made it to the moral argument of such a decision. My heart just would not have allowed it. But now, with this pregnancy that Terry and I both wanted so much, it was the heart of a mother that required me to think about the unthinkable.

My cousin-in-law, Tiffany, who had worked as a neonatal intensive care nurse, stopped by for a visit one day. "Christi, I'm guessing that I know your feelings about ending this pregnancy and I would feel the same way under normal circumstances. But I've seen the other side of this and I feel like I should at least let you know about that part as well. Some of the brain damaged infants that I have cared for suffered horribly. It's heartbreaking. You can tell that they hurt all the time and there's nothing you can do to help or comfort them." She answered some of my questions and we talked for a few minutes. As she was leaving, Tiffany apologized. "I'm not trying to tell you what to do. I just wanted you to have as much information as possible so that you and Terry can make the decision that's right for you. But also keep in mind that that placenta is awfully strong and can do a lot to protect a baby, so don't give up hope!" With that she hugged me and left.

In reality, her words would probably make this decision even harder as morals and emotions could no longer be the deciding factors. I had a child to think of. But at least now, I felt more informed and equipped to make whatever decisions we might have ahead of us.

Terry and I, easily and without hesitation, agreed that we wanted all the information possible before deciding anything. With tests, results, and time, we both felt that we would know what to do if and when a decision needed to be made. We prayed often and hard that God would guide us. Right now though, we had a baby, our baby, who was alive and who deserved to be celebrated! So celebrate we did! With every exam that revealed the baby was growing normally, with every test that didn't show anything out of the ordinary, and when the ultrasound technician told us that we were expecting a girl, we celebrated!

Another daughter! I grew up in a family where I was the only girl in my generation. Brothers and all boy cousins had dominated the scene. Having sisters was inconceivable to me, so I was both surprised and thrilled! Terry didn't seem the least bit disappointed either. We joked about why wouldn't he want to have another girl? He'd get to be the hero again as he was with Ansley. Me, I'm just Mom.

One day, he walked into my hospital room and announced, "I've been thinking, and if this baby is as healthy and perfect as we are claiming she will be, I think we should name her Faith or Hope."

"Oh, I love those names!" I exclaimed, hugging him. Both were already on our girls' names list. At the time that I had scribbled them down, they were in the running because of sounding pretty and being unique. The significance they might end up possessing would have astounded us.

There were some well-meaning family members that had a harder time grasping the true meaning behind those names. They put strong pressure on us, but especially on Terry, to go ahead and end the pregnancy. I never have understood why they wouldn't want to know the results of all of the possible tests first. Perhaps it was a matter of wanting us to take the "safe route" and to do so before we could become entangled in more emotions. It's true that safe routes usually have known outcomes and few surprises along the way. The only problem with that is not all surprises are bad and predictable endings don't leave much room for miracles to take place.

I also couldn't figure out why they were pressuring Terry. He wouldn't make a decision of that nature without me, nor could he without my consent. Maybe they saw him as the one who was better equipped to evaluate and be realistic about the situation and that he could reason with me, or maybe they thought that I shouldn't or couldn't make that kind of choice in my weakened state. Whatever the reason, my heart breaks thinking of my husband having to deal with anyone pressuring him. The man had been making one life-threatening choice after another for the last two weeks, with each call being the right one. His track record was pretty darn good! You would think his decisions would be trusted.

"It's not worth the risk," and "The doctors said..." they pointed out to us. I'm guessing that these family members were convinced that brain damage was certain and why put off the inevitable? It would only get harder. It was eye-opening for me to see how faith is a wonderful thing for people to claim until something important is on the line and it is truly put to the test. Then, suddenly, the safe, easy route really does seem like the best choice to them.

But Terry and I both felt strongly that we owed this baby every chance that she could get. She had fought hard for her little life, defying all odds to this point. What right did we have to deny her any opportunity that there was? How dare we not assume the best possible outcome for her? After all, we had learned that it is okay to believe in miracles.

So Terry found other family members to back him up and then explained one last time, "No! This is a decision that Christi and I will make together after we have all of the information. That's when we'll decide what's the best thing to do for our baby." For the time being, we just needed to be patient and wait. Sometimes a quick decision can be the worst decision of all.

So our daughter stayed where she was and so did I. Going by the doctors' original prediction, I had several months left in my hospital stay. But what had not been factored in was how badly I wanted out of there. I hated that uncomfortable bed, that little room, and I missed my home! Apparently, all of the blood work that had been done had not detected my stubborn gene. How it wasn't noticed remains a mystery to my family. I told everyone that I was planning to be home in time to celebrate my ninth anniversary on September 7th. That would be twenty-four days from the night I had the seizures, and if you asked me, that was long enough. The problem was nobody was asking me. Whenever I volunteered my opinion, people just rolled their eyes where they thought I couldn't see, shook their heads ever so slightly, and politely said things like, "Okay, we'll see. Just remember that it takes a long time to recover from something like this."

The days passed slowly. There were the continuous tests and more pills to take than I could keep track of. Physical therapy was a part of my daily routine as I tried to get mobility back on my left side. It started with riding in a wheelchair as I learned to steady myself while sitting up and with motion. I progressed to using a walker with a little bit of independent walking mixed in. Extreme caution was taken by the therapists because of the pregnancy. With so little control over my limbs and muscles, falls were always a concern. What I still can't figure out is what they were thinking trying to teach a pregnant woman how to walk, or should I say waddle? I guess we have to do the best we can with what we are given to work with.

At some point it was deemed that there was nothing else that could be done for me at the hospital. The rehabilitation team had met their goals, but recommended that I continue therapy after going home. My levels for all of the various tests were as they should be for my condition. The virus had run its course and it was now just a matter of allowing me to recover. Best of all, the neurological tests were not showing any permanent brain impairment, or as my brothers like to say, any new problems. We were cautioned that something might present itself as I reentered the world outside of the hospital. Long-term effects from viral encephalitis can include a number of things such as memory loss, not being able to learn new information, not being able to remember things like phone numbers, fatigue, depression, and mobility problems. Some can last a year or more, some can be permanent. Time would be the best indicator of any problems that we weren't yet aware of.

I did discover one of those neurological issues while still in the hospital. I was washing my face at the sink in my room. Not being able to bathe or shower easily by myself yet, I thought this would feel refreshing and would allow me some much needed independence. I got back into the bed with my face burning. Was I having a reaction to something? Before I had time to do anything, Mom came into the room. Seeing that my face was beet red, she quickly called the nurse. After some investigating and tests, we realized that I was not able to distinguish between hot and cold. Trying to make the water temperature feel comfortable, I kept turning more and more hot water on. I had literally scalded my face! The realization that there wasn't anything more serious going on led us to some stress-relieving laughter over my poor pink cheeks. I quickly made the decision that erring on the side of too cold would be just fine. Looking at this experience as a lesson, I made a mental note to remember that no matter how much information we have or how hard we try to be prepared for what might arise, it will usually be the little, unexpected surprises, the things that nobody knows about or thinks to mention, that we get burned by. I also realized that if something is wrong, if it doesn't feel right, it's best to think through the situation and try to figure out what the problem is or to ask for help before trying over and over again to fix it. I didn't and I literally got myself into hot water.

During my stay, I also found out that in the middle of a crisis, it can be the little things that mean the most. One morning my brother, Scott, was headed to the hospital to visit me. He called on the way and asked me, "Is there anything, and I mean anything, that I can bring you? I'm calling, so you might as well tell me."

I hesitated. What I wanted was just to see him. Somehow the unmerciful teasing I knew I was in for would make me feel as normal as anything else could. Scott had a way of saying what others shied away from and somehow you ended up feeling better afterwards. Yes, I needed to see my brother, but an Egg McMuffin from McDonald's did sound good, so I told him so.

"It's on the way," was all he said.

I was still so weak that my stomach had a hard time handling much solid food, and apparently I needed more time to build up to fast food. It might not have stayed put for long, but that was the best

Egg McMuffin that I have ever had. As Scott wiped my mouth and got me something to drink, it started: "Glad to see you enjoyed it." "Maybe next time I could ask them just to make it into a shake to start with." "Don't even think about asking me for a ribeye."

In that moment, I got my confirmation that the sun would come up tomorrow and that there could be laughter and fun even in the middle of a storm. I learned that when it's the darkest, find something that will make you smile, even if for just a minute or two. That day it was Scott giving me a hard time. The day I stopped driving because of my eyes, it was immersing myself in the radio on my way home.

And find something familiar, comforting, and reassuring, whether it's a brother's teasing, an old t-shirt, a favorite song, or your favorite coffee mug. The point is to have something, anything to make you feel warm and fuzzy and relaxed, to let you see that even in the bad times there can be moments of comfort, safety, and relief.

It might seem as though getting excited over insignificant things could make us feel worse by pointing out all that we don't have to be excited about, as if we are having to settle. But it doesn't work that way. Somehow finding just one good, happy thing makes everything seem better and more hopeful. It is impossible to feel bad at the same time that you are feeling happy, no matter what triggered the happiness. Ask any teenage girl, and a few grown women, if there is anything more fun than getting the giggles for no reason and not being able to stop. You are laughing over nothing and yet, once you get started, every thought that pops into your mind is suddenly a fun one.

My biggest immediate problem was that I didn't have the giggles and having them would have been the only way that I would have seen anything funny about the fact that I was still lying in that dumb hospital bed. The doctors did give me some good news, saying that I was now on my last round of the antiviral medicine that I was being given through the IV. When that series was complete, I would be released. The bad news was that it would take days and possibly a week or more, depending on how fast my body would take it in, putting it after my anniversary deadline.

When that day, September 7th, arrived, Terry and I celebrated in the hospital room with take out food that he had brought with him. I was given a rain check for a dinner at LongHorn Steakhouse, our traditional anniversary restaurant. After we finished eating, we just hugged and hugged, not wanting the sweetness of a moment, that by all accounts should not be taking place, to end. It might not have been the most romantic of our anniversaries, but I could easily argue that it was one of the most special. Finally, Terry headed out saying with a grin, "I'll be back first thing in the morning." Our celebration ended with a very special, "Thank you for today. I love you!"

The next morning he was back, holding my hand as we watched the last drops of the final dose of my medicine flow down the tube and enter my arm. I was going home! I had missed my goal of getting out by one day; that I could live with. As I was wheeled out, I told as many of the medical staff as I saw a heartfelt "Thank you!!!" It's possible that I might have also thrown in a few secret, silent "Told you so!"s, but don't tell my mother.

11

The Recovery

*"Where the loser sees barriers,
the winner sees hurdles."
- Robert Brault*

Being four months pregnant, having a three-year-old, still being extremely weak, and coping with serious mobility issues all contributed to the decision that maybe it would be in everyone's best interest if we camped out at my grandmother's house for awhile before staying at home. The arrangement worked well as she lived by herself in a large home, Mom lived less than a mile away and could stay with Ansley and me during the day while Terry resumed a somewhat normal work schedule. I will always be thankful to God and to Steve, Terry's brother, that Terry was working for Steve during this time and that Steve allowed him the flexibility to be with and take care of me.

I was so eager to be at my own house, but this was the best solution for what we all needed at that moment. I needed help, Ansley needed her mommy and attention, my mom needed to be able to take care of her little girl, my grandmother needed to contribute, and my husband needed some down time while feeling comfortable leaving us. The time would come to return home, but for now, that's not what would help us the most. Sometimes the detours along our routes, although frustrating, are there for our benefit and in the long run, will help us get to where we want to be even quicker.

Whether I was at home or my grandmother's, I was anxious and excited to get back to the joyful mundaneness of my life. I was emotionally and mentally prepared that it would take awhile for things to return to how they had been before the encephalitis. What I didn't understand and, once again, why I'm glad there was no crystal ball to show me too far ahead, was that "how it had been before" was now nothing but a memory. Instead, at least for me, the worst was yet to come. The batteries in my flashlight needed to be fresh because it would take all the energy that I had and a whole lot of patience and perseverance to even make it to the next step on my very dark staircase.

While it had been a rough battle up to this point, the pressure had been on the doctors and the nightmare had belonged to my family; my job had been simply to live. That was about to change. I had just been moved from defense to offense, and what happened next was up to me. The doctors had done their job. My family could and would be worried, supportive, helpful, and loving, but this leg of the journey was mine. The course I took and the outcome from it were my choice and my responsibility. How I emerged from the rough waters that were lying ahead of me would depend largely on the decisions that I made and the disposition I chose to have. It wasn't going to be easy and my life would never again be the same, but just as it had when I was suffering with the loss of my vision, the sun continued to come up each and every morning. This time it just didn't surprise me, and I decided early on that unless I wanted to miss what it was shining on, I had better get up too, no matter what it took.

The month spent at my grandmother's house was meant to get me off to a strong start on the road to recovery by providing rest, help, and a way to get to rehab. I did get lots of help, but the only things that came from the other two goals were strong starts on the road to reality and to learning just how sick I had been and still was.

The worst part of it all was the intense burning, as if my skin was on fire, and the sharp aching pain that the neurological damage caused. Both I felt all over my body. Although it had been pretty bad in the hospital, the medications I was on there must have been masking the severity of the pain. Now it was excruciating! In addition to hurting, I was constantly nauseous, extremely fatigued, and very weak. And none of them had much to do with being pregnant. Needless to say, there was very little that was enjoyable to me. Even resting didn't go so well. The pain kept me awake much of the night and between the nausea, my mobility problems, and being pregnant, it was hard to get comfortable day or night. Life became a game of "Just gotta make it through this day."

My sweet husband got less rest than I did. He

would lay beside me in bed with the television on, watching over me, petrified that I would have a relapse and more seizures. "Thank goodness it was football season. There was usually a game on that I could watch until I fell asleep," he solemnly recalls. In the mornings, he would get up and drive an hour to work. And I thought I was being tough.

The outpatient rehabilitation that I started going to three times a week was another nightmare. I could barely tolerate the twenty minute ride to and from the facility. And once I got there, I had to endure, for the sake of insurance regulations, the insensitive and callous treatment from the very therapists I was counting on to help me get my life back on track. Terry had tried to get me into other rehab programs, but because I was pregnant, none of them would accept me. Not long ago, we were recalling what I had gone through there. Terry got very emotional as he remembered the frustration he felt. "Christi, I tried! I promise, I tried! I wanted to get you into the very best program, but nobody would take you. Once they found out you were pregnant, they just said no. The place you went is the only one that would accept you. I'm so sorry! I promise, I tried."

"I believe you, Sweetheart. I know you did."

In life we have to take the hand of cards we are dealt, look at them, and make a choice: do we play them to the best of our ability or do we pull out of the game? And so, although it might not have been what I was hoping for or expecting, I went to rehab and played the lousy hand I was holding as well as I could.

Believe me when I say the hand stunk! One day I was yelled at by the woman showing me some strengthening exercises. It involved holding my arm out behind my back and pushing against the wall. I was trying my best, but the paralyzation in my shoulder prevented me from holding it in the correct position. Not being able to see behind my back and with my loss of feeling, I couldn't tell if my hand was actually touching the wall or not.

"Geez!" the therapist snapped at me. "Maybe you could try listening to my instructions and do it right next time! Just forget it! You're not even listening, much less trying!" She marched out.

I was too sick to argue back with the feistiness that I normally would have shown and too humiliated to try to explain. I just sat there until someone came into the room and told me where to go next. I swore that I was going to get a t-shirt and write on it with fabric paint, "NOT DUMB, JUST NUMB" to wear to my next appointment. I still regret not having followed through on that idea.

Then there was the woman who ran the tests for vision, hearing, and neurological damage. The vision tests threw her a bit, the neurological tests showed nothing of concern, but the auditory evaluation revealed that there had been some damage, most likely through the nervous system, to the hearing in my left ear. It might or might not improve. A couple of days later, I came in and sat down in her office for another test, I greeted her with, "Good morning. How are you?"

Her return greeting? "Good gosh! Quit talking so loud! This is a small room and I've got a headache! Is there something wrong with you or what?" An appointment was made to discuss the exchange with her and her supervisor. I didn't see her again, but I pray that a senior citizen or a child patient would never receive the same treatment.

Two weeks later, Mom was dropping me off at the front entrance. I struggled out of the front passenger's seat and then opened the rear door to get my walker off of the back seat. Mom asked, "Um, Christi, why are you getting that?"

"They told me that I have to have it. They won't let me move around or do any exercises without it."

"But, Honey, the only place you use it anymore is here."

"I know. I tried to tell them that, but they said that I have to have it."

"Okay," Mom said, "take it in with you then, but leave it folded up and carry it in."

I smiled, shut the car door, and walked in with it hanging off my shoulder and bouncing against my protruding belly like a big metal purse.

When she picked me up a couple of hours later, Mom asked, "So what happened?"

I smiled with a subtle hint of victory. "I walked in carrying the walker and the lead therapist said, 'Well, I guess we'd better find some new exercises for you to do." Mom leaned over to give me a hug and kiss my cheek. She was chuckling softly.

The lack of expectation by the therapists was almost as insulting as their abusive treatment. It's a good thing that I wasn't counting on them to motivate me or I would have been very let down. For instance, they said that I was going to be taught how to tie shoelaces with one hand. "Oh, no, no, no! I don't want to learn how to do it with one hand. I'm here to learn how to use both hands again. That's my goal. Please teach me something to help get the use of my left hand back. That's what I want!" I implored them.

With a huge sigh to emphasize disagreement, I was shown some exercises, but not much time was spent on them. They were too busy having me "practice" making up a twin bed, even after I had explained that this wasn't necessary because each morning I made up the king size bed that I slept in. I was beginning to think that I wasn't the only one with hearing problems. I just did what I was told while there and then went home to do the exercises by myself over and over and over again. It was like playing without a coach, which makes it difficult to win when you are new to the game.

I must confess that I did take immense pride in making up the bed every morning and then putting on my shoes, using both hands to tie them. It might have taken me numerous tries and sometimes up to five minutes to get the bow good enough to stay, but I did it! Yes, this outcome was going to be up to me.

But it wasn't going to be easy. On top of the constant pain, the sickness, and the frustrations with my rehabilitation, the simplest tasks were a struggle. Thankfully, paddling through my vision nightmare had taught me how to adapt and that the old ways aren't necessarily the only ways. I had learned that progress does not necessarily mean that things get easier; it means that you are moving in the right direction.

A shower was exhausting and dangerous, not to mention often too cold. I started asking Terry to get the water going for me whenever possible and I'd just sit down on the shower seat if I needed to catch my breath. Thanks to my lack of balance and my awkward movements, watching me try to get dressed was like watching either a comedy routine or a horror show; take your pick! But I discovered that you can put your clothes on while lying down and that young kids know what they are doing when they sit on the floor to put their pants on. And who says that you can't hook your bra before putting it on? I was so weak that I couldn't hold my toothbrush up and keep it steady with my left hand while squeezing the toothpaste on it with my right, so I would lay it down on the counter to get it ready. Not being able to use my left hand enough to be of any help in blow-drying my hair, Terry rigged up a holder for the dryer by using his guitar stand on the bathroom counter. And I learned that using my grandmother's electrical chair lift to go up and down the stairs, a leftover from her knee surgery, wasn't only safer, but it provided a little extra cuddle time with Ansley when she rode in my lap.

Driving was on hold again because of a six month waiting period after a seizure, but this time that was fine with me. Just getting myself ready to go anywhere was exhausting enough and my concentration in the car was focused on not getting sick. Between all of the doctor appointments and rehab, I had about all of the excitement I needed. There was only so much fun a person could take, so I was happy to leave the driving to my personal chauffeurs and spend my limited energy on getting through the day.

Things were rough where I was, but I knew that somewhere past the horizon, there was something magical, something beautiful, and something well worth paddling hard to reach.

12

The Moments

"Our days are measured in hours,
our lives in moments."
- Christi Kasha

The days melted one into the other. My reward for making it through each one was tucking a little three-year-old into her bed, saying prayers, hugging and kissing her good-night, then getting to lie next to my husband and hearing him say to me, "Thank you for today." Yes, it was a hard period, for me, for Terry, for all of us, but we were making it. And with each tomorrow, I would wake to the sun shining in through the windows, my husband saying, "Good morning, Sunshine!" as he placed his hand on my face, and a little voice calling out, "Mommy, Mommy..." And my survival instincts would once again kick in.

Compared to the previous month that was spent in the hospital, life was somewhat boring. Then the phone call came. It was a conversation that will be with me forever. When I answered and realized what office the call was from, I asked the caller if she could hold for just a moment, then I signaled to Mom and some other family members nearby. They followed me into the sunny, quiet living room where we all sat down. Terry was at work, but what I wouldn't have given to have him there, holding my hand.

"Okay, thank you for waiting. I'm back," I spoke into the handset.

"Yes, Mrs. Kasha, like I said, I'm with Dr. Mann's office at Atlanta Perinatal Consultants. I'm calling about the results of your amniocentesis."

"Okay," was all I could manage to get out. This was the test that would tell us where we stood with the baby's development and brain damage. I couldn't breathe and I felt the blood run from my face, knowing that the next words would affect my life forever.

"Mrs. Kasha, did they tell you what you are having?" the sweet lady on the other end asked.

"We were told that we're having a girl." I was aware that my arms were aching and that one of them was wrapped around my belly.

"No, Mrs. Kasha." There was a slight pause. "You are having a perfectly healthy little girl." Her smile could be heard over the phone.

"Wh...wh...what do you mean?" I wanted to be sure that I had heard correctly.

"Your amnio results all look just like they should. Everything seems to be great! This baby looks as healthy as she can be. The virus never passed through the placenta. Congratulations, Mrs. Kasha. We're so happy for you."

"Thank you! Thank you so much!"

I hung up and I lost it. The days might have been a struggle, the last two months a nightmare, but suddenly it was all worth it. Once more, via the telephone, I had discovered another miracle, a miracle of a lifetime, my baby! Terry rushed home to join the celebration.

"Thank you for today!" he and I said to each other before falling asleep that night, his hand over his baby. I believe both of us might have been saying it more to God than to each other. I hope He heard.

Only a few other moments during the next couple of months could even come close to the joy of that phone call. Although the others may seem trivial in nature, in my memory and in my heart, they hold clues to the true meaning of life to me.

The first moment that comes to mind is my return home. Terry turned the car into our neighborhood of cozy starter homes and I might as well have entered the gates of Heaven. Many times since that day as I have driven down that street, the memory and the emotion of my long awaited return have swept over me. Walking into our cherished home, the only one that Terry and I had shared, I stumbled, literally, from room to room, taking in everything as though I was seeing it for the first time, or maybe understanding that it could be for the last time. A quote by Betty Smith says to look at everything from those two perspectives and "then your time on earth will be filled with glory." Those few moments were.

At the very end of the hallway, I spotted a flat cardboard box hanging on the wall. Written on it with a dark, thick marker, in Terry's handwriting were the words, "Welcome Home." He took it off the wall for me and inside I found a framed print with the Bible verse Isaiah 40:31: "They that wait upon the Lord shall renew their strength, they shall mount up with wings as eagles, they shall run and not be weary, and they shall walk and not faint."

It was a present from Terry to let me know that he believed I would recover and that everything would turn out okay. The picture hung in that spot for the rest of the time that we lived there. The box it came in sits on a shelf at the back of my closet where I see it every day. I keep it there to remind me of what makes a house a home and of the treasures I have in my life.

Sometimes it takes adversity to discover what really matters the most to us. A house catches on fire and what the owner rushes to save will reveal his true "valuables." The same thing is true with our lives. When we see smoke, we will race to save what is most important to us. It might be a relationship, our career, financial security, our reputation, our children, peace of mind, or opportunity. What we find might be positive and comforting, or it could be a wake up call that our "valuables" need reevaluating. For me, I was home, with my husband and my child. I was where I belonged.

Another moment that stands far apart from other day-to-day happenings took place at a K-Mart. Terry, Ansley, and I were there shopping. Ansley started asking to get out of the buggy she was riding in. As Terry lifted her up, I held out my arms to hold her. He handed her to me ever so easily and I stood there just holding her in both arms for a moment. Then I took a few cautious steps before putting her down. She was busy looking at all of the holiday decorations and didn't notice my tears, but Terry did. "Are you okay?" he asked. I knew that he was checking on both my physical and emotional state.

"Yes, I'm wonderful!" I answered gratefully.

He realized what had just taken place and pulled me to him in a celebratory hug. It was the first time that I had carried my little girl since I went into the hospital. I was extremely wobbly when I walked, often needed assistance, and had very little endurance, but I had grown strong enough to hold Ansley. I wasn't where I wanted to be, but if I looked behind me I could see just how far I had come. I had gone from having someone hold my eyelids open to being able to hold my daughter. It wasn't much, but for that moment, it was everything. And in it, I found enough hope to get me to the next precious moment, and another reason to keep paddling.

That reason couldn't have come at a better time. Everything was extremely hard, both physically and emotionally, and I wasn't improving as quickly as I had hoped. I was very pregnant, very tired, and in constant pain. My life was one frustrating, exhausting moment after another. It wasn't that I didn't have help, but these were things that no one could fix. Father Time was in charge now. This part of my journey was a lesson in determination. I couldn't control the makeup or the span of the clouds or the direction of the wind. But I could take action and continue fighting to get to where I wanted to be.

The pregnancy was still going well, but it can be a struggle to keep up with the demands of carrying a baby under normal circumstances. I carry large and straight out in front. With the balance issues I had, this didn't help matters much. Maintaining the nutritional requirements was a nightmare. I still had trouble keeping food down. My goal each evening was to wait long enough before vomiting to allow my medicines and vitamins time to be absorbed. The doctor said an hour should do the trick. I would set the timer after taking all of my pills each night. It was the anti-seizure medicine that made us the most nervous. After the timer went off, Terry and I could relax and enjoy the rest of the evening. Sometimes I would be bold and daring and would try other foods, but my safest staples were a certain brand of nutritional shakes, peanut butter and jelly sandwiches, and ice cream. Even with that diet, I ended up having a net gain of only four pounds during the pregnancy, thanks to the constant nausea and having lost about twenty-five pounds while in the hospital.

It was the pain that was the hardest to cope with. The burning sensation that ran throughout my body, as though the underside of my skin was on fire, was caused by the lesions on my brain left from the virus. Somehow my nerve fibers were affected. I now have a different understanding and the utmost admiration for people with terminal illnesses and the physical pain that can be a result. There was an elderly couple I met when I was receiving my steroid treatments for my optic nerve. The wife had been very ill with some disease that caused chronic pain. The husband, her caretaker, was diagnosed with cancer. He sat next to me for several days while receiving his chemotherapy treatments. The husband's love for his wife of many years was obvious as we talked. He wasn't worried about himself, he was terrified about who would take care of her if he couldn't. Several weeks later, I happened to hear a local news story and knew, because of the address, that it was this precious couple they were reporting on. The man and woman had ended their lives together because the chemo wasn't helping his cancer and the thought of her living in her condition without him was unbearable to either of them.

Whether I agree or disagree with their decision is irrelevant; I simply understand the why. I was coping because I always had the hope that tomorrow would be better than today. But even at that, there were moments while Terry was driving us somewhere that I would make sure the doors were locked. I had moments of terror that I might suddenly decide that I just couldn't stand it anymore and would try to end it by throwing myself out of the car. I know now that one of the side effects of the anti-seizure medicine I was taking is suicidal thoughts, but at the time, those moments of panic were horrible. Thankfully, the moments of hope and love won out.

My hearing was also affected by the lesions. Background noises were painfully loud to me. The noise from a ceiling fan was deafening and torturous. The hum of the florescent bulb above the kitchen sink was so intrusive that it would keep me from falling asleep on the sofa in the next room. Even the simple act of turning my head on the pillow was agonizing because the noise of the soft fabric rubbing against my ear was amplified. Thank heavens regular, prominent noises like the radio, the television, people talking, or the squeals of a little girl didn't bother me and helped to counter the miserable moments of both the days and nights.

I often ended up spending the night on the sofa. Thanks to my growing belly, I had an easier time getting comfortable there. Not that I necessarily got more sleep, but if I was going to be awake, I might as well be as comfortable as possible. Terry, in his quiet way of making my life a little easier, would spread out my favorite blanket on the sofa each night before we went to bed, so that it would be ready for me if I needed it. When I did stay all night in our bed, I would often lie awake for hours on end, passing the time by playing what I termed "clock math" with my "easy-to-read" alarm clock, a gift from Terry that now sat on my bedside table. As its large, bright numbers changed, I would make mathematical equations out of each set of numbers. 2:36 represented $2 \times 3 = 6$. 4:29 would translate into a numerical sequence: $4 \times 2 = 8$ and the next number is 9. When I told Terry about my technique to pass the time, he responded, "Um, that's not normal."

"Since when have I..."

"Never mind," he interrupted. "We won't go there. Hey, if it works..."

The games helped me make it through the nights. The mornings brought their own struggles. Terry would usually find me sitting on the sofa, wrapped in the blanket, crying from the pain. I just hurt so badly! After bringing me my medicines and a nutritional shake, he would quietly sit holding me until he had to go to work. My husband has said that it just about killed him to leave me like that, but the reality was there wasn't anything that he could do to make it better. He'd kiss me goodbye, making me promise that I would call him if I needed anything. Then he would leave. And life would go on.

Not being able to do the same activities with Ansley that we had done before would have been extremely depressing except for the fact that most of the time all I really felt like doing was curling up in a hole somewhere. I was too sick to even be upset and down over my situation or to question why I had survived and why I had to go through this. In the years since, there have been many times that I have thought, and occasionally even gone so far as to verbalize, "It would have been better if I had just died, not just for me, but for Terry and Ansley." Yes, I had lived, but living wasn't the same as feeling alive.

But some things are worth the pain, effort, and time. So I learned to cling to and treasure those precious moments that made my life worthwhile.

13

The Confusion

*We do not see things as they are,
we see them as we are.*
-The Talmud

    Whether you are going through a storm or watching a friend or loved one go up against one, the whole process can be confusing. Whichever side you are on, it's often difficult to know what will help or if help is even an option. How many times have we said or heard other people say, "I want to do something for her (or him), but I don't know how I can help"?

    For those of us facing adversity, most of the time we don't mind accepting help and we're thankful when it comes. The problem is often that we don't know what to ask for or that we do know what we need isn't something that can be given to us. For me, what I needed was my life back, and the more help that I accepted, the more elusive that would become. Someone who is struggling financially needs money, but resources may not be available or the person doesn't want one more debt to worry about. Yes, often the only way to really get through a storm is to paddle through it ourselves; no one else can do it for us.

My circumstances were somewhat unique, making it that much more difficult for anyone to know how to help. On top of that, even the people closest to me had a hard time comprehending just how sick I still was and how horrible I felt. I wasn't trying to hide my misery from anyone, I just didn't realize until years later that they didn't understand. Even if I had known, I'm not sure that I had the energy to try to explain it in detail.

It must have been confusing to those around me. Compared to where I'd started from in the ICU or even as I left the hospital, I was a thousand times better, but I was hardly even a reflection of the person that I used to be. I was up and functioning independently, but in addition to my major and more obvious handicaps, the damage to my nerves had left me with a variety of conflicting, and oftentimes amusing, problems. My body ached and burned, but you could tap me on the left side of my back and I wouldn't be able to feel it. If you gently caressed my skin, it felt as though you were giving me a deep massage, but I was no longer even remotely ticklish. I couldn't control my left arm as I lifted it up, but when I walked, it wouldn't swing at all unless I intentionally made it do so. Walking was less painful than standing and snapping my fingers hurt my lower back. Activities that seemed as though they would have been easy and enjoyable weren't at all, while things that would normally fall into the work or strenuous category were what I craved, and the things that people worried about were the least of my concerns. But while it was hard to understand, it was even harder to try to explain.

My godmother, Donna, once invited my grandmother, my mom, and me to her house for lunch. Mom couldn't understand my reluctance to go. She knew how much I thought of Donna and she thought it would do me good to get out. "Yeah, right," I remember thinking. "Could you just shoot me in the head instead? I would probably enjoy that more." But appreciating Donna's offer to do something sweet for me, I decided to go. Getting ready, the ride over, and even having to tune into the conversation was so physically exhausting that I couldn't enjoy the afternoon.

Precious church friends would bring dinner over to our house. We begged the members of the congregation who were coordinating the meal delivery to have people bring the food to Terry's parents' house for Terry to pick up there. But not understanding the need for this, they just couldn't bring themselves to do it. To them, especially being older, asking people not to come over seemed as though I was being ungrateful. I was even told that "Sometimes being a good Christian means letting other people be good Christians."

When they wouldn't give, I did. Our friends were being so thoughtful that I didn't have much of a choice. I appreciated their generosity, but it was a nightmare to me. Visitors meant that I was going to use up much of my strength getting dressed, brushing my teeth and hair, making sure Ansley was at least presentable, and that the place was picked up enough for them to have a path to walk into the kitchen to put the food down and a spot to sit. All of that when just going down the five steps to open the front door was hard for me to manage and often caused me to stumble. And we won't even get into the embarrassment factor of having people watch me try to walk. Although I loved seeing my friends, it took more effort than I would have ever thought just to carry on a conversation. People would compassionately stay to visit, not knowing that I was fervently praying that I wouldn't get sick in front of them. If someone wasn't staying, the food was usually handed to me at the door and the person would stand there to talk, which was so hard for me to do. I would have asked them to come in, but you know how those at-the-door visits often end up lasting longer than you plan. After the friend left, I would have to make several difficult trips up and down the stairs because I could only carry one thing at a time.

The thoughtfulness and the generosity meant so much to us. The problem was that I was fighting for my life and it was taking all of my strength to do the things that would help me to survive this storm.

People want to help, but what survival means and entails can be a matter of perspective. So if someone asks if or how they can help you through your adversity, but you really aren't sure what you need, my suggestion would be to tell them, "Yes! You know what I need? I need people to cheer me on and to just listen when I'm down. I wish that other people could fight this battle for me, but I have to do for myself. And right now, how I feel can change from one minute to the next, so it's hard to say anything specific. But encouragement would be wonderful! Can I call you?" The answer you receive will let you know if that person's number should be on speed dial.

On the other hand, if you are the person wanting to offer assistance, swap the words around and try this, "Listen, I know you are going through a lot right now and I'd love to help. If there's something that would make your life easier, like taking the kids for a couple of hours, bringing you dinner, vacuuming the house, yard work, anything like that, let me know and I'll coordinate getting it done. But sometimes people just need someone to vent to and bounce thoughts off of. Please know that you can call me anytime for that. I might not know the answers, but I can listen. And sometimes people just need their space. If that's the case, say the word and I'll put out the "Do Not Disturb" bulletin. But you have to let me call you for thirty seconds every couple of days just to make sure nothing's changed." Oh, what I would have given if I had known how to make that kind of exchange happen and how happy some of my friends would have probably been to not have to cook for another family.

During a storm, the greatest help can simply be knowing that help is available. And the greatest strength is rarely the strength of others, but the strength in ourselves that others can help us find.

14

The Lessons of the Game

*"If we knew the outcome,
the game would no longer be fun."
- Christi Kasha*

My mind goes back to a soccer game that I was playing in when I was about thirteen years old. My father was the coach. Suddenly in the middle of the game, he pulled me out of my offensive position. I didn't need a rest, but he was good about rotating players, so I didn't think twice about it. I got something to drink, caught my breath, and stood beside him watching the game.

"You rested?" he asked, without taking his eyes off the field.

"Yeah, I'm good." I was ready to get back in.

"Okay, then go put on the extra keeper's jersey. I'm putting you in at goal."

"But, Dad, you can't!" I strongly protested, "I've never even practiced there! I have no idea what to do!" Panic rushed over me.

"Look, you're aggressive and that's what I need in that position. And as far as what you need to do, let me explain it to you: stop the ball! Now go over there and get ready. You are going in at the next substitution." He was using his coach's voice. There was no point in arguing.

So stop the ball I did, many, many times during the next five years as the team's starting goalie, including our State Championship season. I took away from the game that day, and from the hundreds of others that I spent standing in front of the goal, much more than the trophies, pride, bruises, skinned knees, and wonderful friendships. I came off of those fields carrying with me valuable lessons, lessons that I would need more than my favorite coach could have foreseen.

I discovered how to win and how to lose, both with dignity. I was taught never to give up or to take something that seems easy for granted because the outcome of a game isn't certain until it's over. I found out that some shots you just can't stop, no matter how badly you want to, some will be easy to block, some you'll just plain miss, and if you play long enough, you will see that once in awhile, against all odds, something amazing happens. I learned that "going for it" can leave you hurting and bruised, but that the pain is nothing compared to the thrill of doing what you're there to do. I quickly discovered that winning sometimes means defying all common sense. There is nothing logical about throwing yourself onto the hard ground or diving in front of a kicker's feet. But if I wanted victory, that just might be what it would take. I found out that fields can be very different and can have a great impact on how you need to play and on the outcome of the game. Some are flat, smooth, soft, and predictable, while others are hard, rough, and rocky, causing the ball to do unexpected things and making it easy to get hurt. But regardless, you have to play by giving it your all while making minor adjustments for the conditions. A tougher field doesn't require playing with less enthusiasm, it means that you play to get ahead quickly. The worse the terrain, the more difficult a comeback can be.

Perhaps, most importantly, my dad sending me in as goalie that very first time taught me that you don't have to always know ahead of time exactly what to do or how to do it perfectly. You just have to know why you are doing it. And then you simply need to get in the game, follow your gut, and do the best you can with the attributes that you have. I don't remember whether we won or lost that game. My guess would be that we lost, as we did a lot of that during that period. What I do remember is having fun in my new position and walking off the field happy, excited, and feeling as though I had just accomplished something. In the end, shouldn't that be the reason for us to play, no matter what game we are in? I thank God and my coaches for the hands-on education I received on those fields. It would be needed for the most important game of all, and it would allow me to run on and off life's playing fields feeling good about my journey and myself.

15

The Fight

"Pain is temporary. It may last a minute, an hour, a day, or a year, but eventually it will subside and something else will take its place. If I quit, however, it lasts forever."
- Lance Armstrong

As I saw it, I was staring at two possible outcomes: this disease could beat me or I could beat it. Period. I had come too far to give up now, especially in a game that had a whole lot more time left on the clock. Somewhere deep inside, I understood that it was going to take a lot of determination, hard work, pain, and pure, raw emotion, but I didn't see there being a choice. How I was going to make things better, I didn't know nor did I stop to think about. I just knew what I was fighting for.

There were two precious little girls who were counting on me and a husband who had sacrificed so much. What was I going to tell them? "Sorry, you just weren't worth the effort. It was too hard and hurt too much." No, that was not an option. If I had anything to say about it, and as long as I was conscious, then I did. Terry, Ansley, and I were going to smile and laugh again and our new baby would grow up in a home filled with love, not sorrow. The disease had taken many things from me, some that I would probably never reclaim, but I refused to let it rob my family or me of our joy. Giving up or giving in would have done just that.

This storm had shaped my life, but I'll be damned if I was going to it define me! No, this game wasn't over, it was just getting started, and it was time to run onto the field, go with my gut, and play with my heart.

It was the "going with my gut" strategy that caused me to do many things and act in ways that did not make logical sense to those nearest me as they watched me struggle. I was a constant source of frustration to my poor mother. The fact that I rarely behaved as she thought I should worried her to no end. She and others were scared that I was pushing myself too hard. To some extent, they were right, I was pushing myself. I had to, otherwise I might have remained under those dark skies forever and I was scared that nothing would ever get any better. Losing hope, as I had discovered with my vision, can be dangerous. I couldn't afford to risk doing that again and I needed to see some sort of progress to ensure that I kept going.

Playing with your heart doesn't always go hand-in-hand with logic and reasoning either. Logic would have said that I should rest and sleep as much as possible while recovering and that I should accept any and all offers of help. Cautious reasoning would have prevented many, many falls. Just for the record, falling while pregnant isn't always as dangerous as we believe. If you do it often enough, you learn how to fall and land without getting hurt, even on stairs. I became a professional. However, I strongly advise against doing so in front of anyone. It might put the health of family members who witness such events in jeopardy. I learned to keep quiet about the number of spills I took. Terry now will just simply say, "I don't want to know, do I?"

"No, Sweetheart, trust me, you don't."

Mom would often come over to visit and I would proceed to drive her crazy by insisting on doing things for myself. She would beg me to let her carry baskets of laundry up and down the stairs for me. I would refuse and she would sit there holding her breath and shaking her head. Offers to do the dishes would result in me telling her, "No thanks." She would try to wait on me; I'd beat her to the kitchen. I know that it must have been hard on my mother to watch her child struggle so. And struggle I did.

My balance was so off and my gait so unsteady that every step I took was uncertain. "Running up and down the stairs" meant slowly taking one cautious step at a time while leaning against the wall for balance and support. Unloading the dishwasher required holding onto the counter with one hand and removing just a few things at a time with the other. I wasn't strong or coordinated enough to lift up but a few items into the cabinets at once. Racing Mom to the kitchen often turned into her squealing in horror as I tripped over my own feet, almost falling, or bumped into a piece of furniture on the way.

It's true that had I used more caution, we would not had nearly as many broken dishes or spots on the carpet from spills. Sensibility would have dictated that I consider talking to the doctor to find out if there was some type of pain medicine that I could take. Common sense would have required that I turn over my Children's Ministry duties to someone else. Rational thinking would have meant keeping the cleaning service that my dad and stepmom were paying for instead of deciding that I wanted to start doing it myself again. There was no denying that I could have pushed myself less and made my life easier.

The problem was that easier was not what I needed the most. I needed hope and I needed confidence. I needed them more than I needed rest or to not hurt, more than unbruised skin or looking graceful. I needed them not for my physical health, but for my emotional well-being. Each time I did a load of laundry by myself, cleaned the bathroom, or got Mom something to drink instead of her getting it for me, I gained just a little bit of confidence. Taking medication for the pain might have helped temporarily, but I needed the hope that one day it would be gone. In order to find that hope, I had to monitor the pain to see if it was getting any better, and the only way to do that was to feel it. I might have been a klutz, but the only hope that I had of one day being stronger and getting my balance back was to risk the falls.

Besides, easier was often more painful. Sitting around just thinking about how pathetic my situation was didn't help the pain, it only drew attention to it. It was when I was focusing on or doing something that I valued that I felt the pain the least. The physical healing would come with time, and if it didn't, at least the hope, confidence, and happiness that I would find along the way would give me a reason to leave this game with a smile on my face.

Yes, I knew why I was playing. I might not have been able to walk without a limp, much less wear the high heels that I loved so much. I didn't have the strength to stroll along the peaceful nature trail, not to mention running up and down the soccer fields. Eating dinner now meant knocking something over at almost every meal, needing someone to cut up my meat for me, and counting on others to tell me when I had food on my face since I couldn't feel it. But these limitations didn't mean that I had to give up on my dreams and goals. I was bound and determined that I was still going to be the mom that I had always wanted to be and that I would do what I could to make a difference in this world, whenever and however I could, no matter how insignificant it seemed. I might have been a mess, but I had been blessed beyond measure. God had done His part and my family had done theirs. It was now time for me to do mine. If it was hard, if it was sad, if my legs hurt, if people stared, and my pride got bruised, it would be worth it. I had something much more valuable on the line, I had something to push for and somewhere to push towards. And I had love on my side.

Quickly I discovered that my best course of action was to get moving, in more ways than one. Waking up in pain each morning, I learned to force myself to get up and, as soon as I could, take a shower or jump into the tub. Well okay, maybe not jump. It took effort, but something about the water on my skin stimulated my nerves and got my blood flowing. It wasn't unusual for me to have to sit down on the bed afterwards to catch my breath. But whether it was from the water, the heat, the movement, or all three of them combined, the pain was not as intense afterwards and I would feel more energized, which was helpful because I had things to do.

Things of importance awaited me, like caring for my extremely bright and full of life three-year-old. My love for that little girl motivated me to take on tasks that I didn't feel like doing. She had suffered more than any little angel should have to suffer. Now she needed her mommy and as much of a normal life as possible. There would be another little one making her appearance soon and I wanted to be physically strong enough to take care of her too. Giving Ansley a bath, dressing her, fixing meals, playing, and cleaning up all caused me to use my muscles and gain more strength, energy, and mobility. In many ways, Ansley was taking care of me more than I was taking care of her.

Love has a way of doing that. Ever notice how whenever we put ourselves on the giving end instead of the receiving end of things, we feel better. Perhaps it was just a matter of having something else to focus on. But more likely, it is the power of love in action.

Our Sunday mornings are a good example of that. They were our busiest time of the week. I continued to help with the children's programs at church and Terry with the music. I was on my feet a lot, but seemed to hurt less. I don't remember many times that I was ready to go home. Why would I be? The kids there didn't seem to care how I walked. They were more interested in laughing and hugging, and I found joy looking at their sweet faces and innocent, happy eyes. Yes, we were giving, but we received so much more in return. Being with the kids and among friends was as healing as any medicine could have ever been. Both gave me more strength and more reasons to keep fighting my way through this storm. Those few hours gave me a chance to see the sun peeking through the clouds and gave me hope that things would get better. And they did.

16

The Celebrations

*"Pain is inevitable,
misery is optional."
- Hyrum Smith*

Celebrations can come in many forms and can be held for everything from major milestones to small, magical moments. They can be planned or happen spontaneously. They can be public or private. Celebrations are not only what we do after surviving a storm, they are often what helps us get through the storm. They are a reminder that there is still happiness, goodness, and beauty even in the middle of adversity.

Most of the celebrations that took place during this period were small, private moments that would have seemed inconsequential under normal circumstances. But life is a matter of perspective and from our point of view, they were worthy of getting excited over and could involve both laughter and tears of happiness.

Terry came home one day and stopped just inside the front door. Wynonna Judd's version of

"Testify to Love" was blaring on the CD player and I was singing and dancing, waving both of my hands in the air to the best of my ability. I didn't hear him come in or realize that he was there watching me stagger around. What Terry was witnessing was a celebration of love.

I have loved that song since the first time I heard it, but the lyrics about how every word of our story is a testimony to love and how with every breath we can give thanks to God now had a greater meaning to me as they reflected what I was feeling. For those few minutes, the pain and the struggles didn't matter. All I felt was thankfulness for the love that I had received and that I wanted to give back, and my overwhelming love for life. Terry stood there until I finished, just taking in my heartfelt worship and celebrating with tears of joy how far I had come. Rarely does a day go by without me listening to that song as a reminder to celebrate and to love.

Many of the other celebrations we shared were almost silly, but nonetheless a testimony of where we had come from. I ran to the phone one afternoon, "Terry!" I squealed with joy.

"What is it?" he reciprocated my excitement.

"I opened a can! I did it, Terry, by myself, with the electric can opener!" For the first time, my arm was strong enough to hold the can up in the right position. I was crying and, although I couldn't prove it, it sounded like he was too.

Another day, Terry walked into the bathroom and his mouth dropped open. "You look beautiful!" He wrapped his arms around me, then pushed me back to arms-length so that he could look at me. "I've missed seeing your hair pulled up. I love it!" It was the first time that I had managed to get my hair up in a ponytail. A few years earlier, I would have never believed that I would have heard those words ever coming out of his mouth.

There were other kinds of celebrations too, like the sighs of relief Terry would let out when he realized that I was okay after a fall. Or when, despite my weakened muscles and the pregnancy, I would make it to the bathroom, especially in a public place, before having an accident. But in my mind, the most important celebration of all would happen every night as Terry and I would say a prayer together thanking God for what we had, asking Him for the strength to do what we needed to do, and for His guidance in knowing what that was. Terry would end by placing his hand on my very large belly and saying, "Perfect baby, God." Then to each other, the words, "Thank you for today. I love you. Good night," were exchanged as we celebrated love.

Some celebrations were much more public, like the one that took place at church during a worship service. Not being able to see their faces clearly, Terry told me afterwards that as I was singing the praise hymns, I had raised my hands into the air as an act of worship that was not unusual for that service. I didn't realize what I had just done, but some of the choir members did. They began crying as they witnessed me raising my left arm for the first time in many months.

Another Sunday, a friend came up to me and

said, "Christi, every time I see you walk in, I thank God for your limp." I'm sure that my expression begged for a further explanation. He continued with a smile, "It reminds me that He still performs miracles."

Yes, celebrations can help us continue to fight our way out of the storm. But sometimes they are the reasons that we decided to fight so hard in the first place.

One cold Sunday afternoon in February, I left church with a friend who was sweet enough to drive me across town to the baby shower that was being given for me at my grandmother's house. I was sitting in the den talking with the family members and friends that had come to celebrate this baby. As I stood up to go get something else to drink from the other room, I heard someone say, "Christi, I think you sat in something. The back of your dress is wet."

"What?" I twisted around. I hadn't felt anything, but my nerve damage might have caused me to not be able to sense the wetness in the same way that it was often hard for me to tell if a load of laundry was completely dry. Having had more than one accident during this ordeal, I guessed what had happened, and I was, to put it mildly, horrified that I had wet myself at my shower. The evidence was pretty clear. Sure enough, there was a huge wet spot on the back of my dress and no spills where I had been sitting. Bravely I said, "I guess it's a good thing that I brought a change of clothes. I'll be right back. Sorry, y'all."

Tiffany, my cousin, the neonatal nurse who had

talked to me about the decision we faced with the pregnancy, offered to come help me. We went into the bathroom. Once we were in the smaller closed space, Tiffany started grinning, "Christi..."

"Yeah?"

"Um... this smells like amniotic fluid." She held my clothes closer and sniffed. "Yep, I'm very familiar with that smell and this is definitely amniotic fluid. Your water just broke!"

"What?" It was two weeks before my due date.

"We've got a baby coming!"

She helped me clean up and change clothes, and we went back downstairs. There was quite a bit of excitement in the room and plenty of comments about how this was one way to get people to remember your baby shower. A lot of work had gone into this party and I wanted everyone to be able to enjoy it, so I sat back down. "I'm not having any contractions or pain, so let me at least open my gifts before I have to go."

I started the unwrapping process and was enjoying "oohhing and aahhing" over the wonderful presents. This didn't go over so well with my guests. I was strongly advised to hurry it up. Labor with Ansley had lasted sixteen hours and now there was nothing going on that made me feel we needed to rush, so I continued on. It didn't take long before I discovered that I had been overruled. In between presents I noticed that a couple of the women were on the floor off to the side. I wondered what they were doing. Then I saw that they were saving time by unwrapping the remaining gifts before handing them to me.

Realizing that I was fighting a losing battle, I gave in and left with Mom to go home. The contractions started on the way and Terry and Ansley met us in the driveway to head to the hospital for one indescribable celebration!

Faith Ann Kasha was born five hours later! She was perfect, beautiful, and completely healthy! She weighed seven pounds on the nose. The vaginal delivery went smoothly and easily, thanks to the help of an epidural, and there were no complications whatsoever. But the birth was slightly unusual in circumstances.

Terry was going out to the waiting room to let our families know that we were ready to start pushing and to get my mom and dad, who were planning to be in there with us. As he was walking out, I said, "Terry, both of our moms and my dad have been in delivery rooms during births, but I know that your dad has never seen a baby being born. Please tell him that he is welcome to come in if he wants to."

"Okay, that's sweet. I'll tell him you said so."

Almost as an afterthought, my voice followed him as he walked out, "And tell anyone else who wants to come in, that they're welcome, too."

I guess being incapacitated and in the hospital for a month has a way of making you lose your modesty. It's a good thing because our families took me seriously! A couple of minutes later, I looked up to see a parade of people, including Terry's dad, walking into the room. Eight members of our family were there to witness and celebrate our daughter's birth with us. Well, if anyone had earned a celebration, it was Faith!

Our sweet midwife let Terry be the one to deliver his little girl. With tears in his eyes, he placed our perfect baby in my arms. Many years later, I confessed that that moment was one of the scariest of my whole life. "What if I can't hold her? What if I drop her? What if I can't take care of her? What if I'm not strong enough?" all raced through my mind instantaneously. Those fears dissipated fairly quickly as I readjusted her little body securely in my arms and nuzzled her to my breast, where she took to nursing immediately. As I stared down at the beautiful gift that I was holding, this tiny answer to so many prayers, I wasn't seeing her as the miracle that she was. I was only seeing love.

Then my precious baby was taken from me by her daddy and placed in the arms of her mesmerized big sister who had just been brought into the room. Moved by the sight of my two beautiful children just staring at each other and by my overwhelming love for both of them, I understood in a heartbeat that sometimes the greatest joys are those that follow the darkest nights.

I thought of the name that we had chosen, Faith, and the bible verse that I had memorized many years earlier, "For faith is the substance of things hoped for, the evidence of things not seen." (Hebrews 11:1, KJV) Yes, we had picked the right name. "Please, God, let it always remind us to celebrate the blessings, even those that we haven't laid eyes on yet."

17

The Choices

"The road we are on is not always our choice, but how we view the scenery along the way is a decision that we make daily."
- Christi Kasha

Two days later we took our baby home to see what new challenges and magical moments life's currents would bring our way. It didn't take me long to figure out that while the storm might have passed and the sun was shining in our faces, the waters remained rough and it would take a lot more work to get to where I wanted to be. Almost everything was still a physical challenge and my impairments were even more obvious as I compared the difficulty that I had doing things now versus three years earlier when Ansley was an infant. Back then I had felt like I was playing dolls the way I had as a child. With Faith, there was nothing recreational about the tasks of motherhood. Changing diapers often hurt my arm, as holding little legs up would call for me to keep it in what was now an uncomfortable position. Getting those sweet little clothes on had gone from playing dress up to real work, and buttoning tiny buttons was next to impossible. At least now

I had a valid excuse for running late everywhere. Each movement that I made while holding Faith had to be deliberate; I couldn't just tuck her under my arm or balance her on my hip and go.

Ansley's needs were harder to tend to also, but at least she was big enough to do many things on her own and to help out with others. The most difficult change for the two of us was that my new disabilities combined with a new baby sister prevented us from being able to do many of the things that we had enjoyed just six months, six long months, earlier.

I guess that I could have become depressed, moped around, and claimed that it was all too much to handle, and no one would have blamed me. But I didn't have the time or the desire to complain. I had too much to do and too much to be thankful for. I was living my dream; well, my dream with a few alterations to it. It was tough, very tough, but tough is not the same as too hard and it's a long way from impossible. We would just have to find new things to do and get busy making new memories. I didn't want to suffer any more than necessary, but I had discovered that other types of pain can hurt worse than physical discomfort. Life involves changes whether we are handicapped or not. We might as well be an active part of them. Sitting on the shore, watching the waves roll in is nice and relaxing, and sometimes we need that. But just watching isn't nearly as exciting as riding the waves in or letting them break on top of you.

Thankfully, I received proof that my physical

situation wasn't stagnant and that things were improving. This new found hope helped to keep my spirits and determination up. My body must have been giving everything to take care of my baby and there wasn't much left for me. Now that I was no longer pregnant, it could start tending to itself and the recovery process sped up.

The morning after having Faith, I woke up and noticed something strange. For the first time in six months, turning my head against the pillow didn't bother me and background noises seemed normal again. Maybe she had been lying against a nerve or maybe it was my body's way of jump-starting itself to getting back on track. I also found that I had more energy and slept better. The best part happened gradually. One day it hit me that the horrific, burning pain wasn't just better, it was gone! It had dissipated a little at a time, but I had been so busy that I hadn't been gauging it. An aching, overworked muscles, pulled-something, kind of discomfort had taken its place. Having played sports, I could handle that. The icing on the cake came a week and a half after Faith's birth. My doctor gave me the go-ahead to start driving again. "Look out world! Here I come!" I chose for my mantra. I was still a physical disaster, but that would be the case no matter what I was doing, so I figured I might as well be doing something worthwhile. Discovering just how precious life is and how quickly a storm can come upon us made doing the things that I loved and that might make a difference that much more important to me.

My family, primarily Mom, would once again worry that I was taking on and attempting to do too much. It was even brought up that I might be in denial of my circumstances and limitations. They didn't need to be concerned. I wasn't in denial. It would have been nearly impossible to dismiss or ignore what I was going through when every minute of the day there was something to remind me of the truth. Whether it was my arms hurting from getting Faith in and out of her car seat, getting winded from walking up and down the aisles, having to use a magnifying glass to find the right kind and amount of meat that I needed, sticking my head inside the freezer doors because I couldn't read the vegetable labels from the outside, being asked to reslide my credit card at the checkout payment box because I had pushed the wrong button, trying to get out of the store before losing control of my bladder, taking in from the car the refrigerated groceries first in case I was too worn out to bring in all of the bags, or dozens of other things, a simple shopping trip was a reality check of my disabilities. Yeah, there was very little chance of me being in denial.

However, being very busy was a correct assumption. I was definitely that, but not because I was pushing myself to try to prove something, as was the family concern. It wasn't even out of obligation to the special promise I made each night. At some point during our prayers together, Terry or I one would say the words, "As for me and my house." We were referencing the Bible verse, "As for me and my household, we will serve the Lord." (Joshua 24:15, NIV) It was our reminder and renewal of our promise and commitment to God that we would serve Him in any way that He needed. I wanted to keep that promise, yes, but my busyness was more a factor of having fun doing what I loved. For me, that meant working with kids and young people and helping those in need. For Terry, it was music.

Isn't it funny how when God is included, opportunities and gifts have a way of finding each other? Because of changes going on at our church, one door after another after another opened up and I found myself not only serving as the chairman of Children's Ministries, but also teaching children's choir, children's classes on Wednesday evenings and Sunday mornings, overseeing the acolytes, directing Vacation Bible School, and serving on various other committees. I loved every minute of it! At about this same time, Terry went from just playing guitar for our praise team to directing it while playing guitar, singing, and leading the worship service, all at the same time. The joke used to be that our children thought they lived at church and visited home, considering the amount of time that we spent there. We might have been "serving," but we received far more than we ever gave and happiness was a given in our lives

Having been through tragedy, it became more important than ever for me to help in other ways as well. I savored the chance to donate blood and platelets to the American Red Cross. There was something haunting to me about the thought of family members sitting at a hospital where a loved one was critically ill, having to worry about needing to donate themselves because the blood bank is low. That should never have to happen. What if that patient needed them at his bedside, telling him to not give up? A few hours seemed a small sacrifice of my time. I qualified, so what excuse did I really have, that I didn't feel good? Well, too bad; someone out there felt worse than me.

On Tuesday evenings at the downtown church where my father was the pastor, I started supervising the inner city teens who got together for pizza and fellowship. Ansley and Faith were able to go to the playground with their grandfather while I got to hang out with some really special teenagers who were not only fun, but also inspiring to be around. One night the girls braided Ansley's hair into cornrows. Talk about an excited little girl! That hair didn't come down for a week! What a special period in my life of giving, receiving, and learning. If this time made even a fraction of the difference in the life of someone else as it did in my own, I will be forever grateful.

But my greatest and most fulfilling happiness didn't come from the time I spent helping out with those programs. They couldn't hold a candle to the fun that I had doing things with my girls, simple activities that brought us tons of laughter, joy, and memories. We would go on breakfast picnics at nearby playgrounds, play miniature golf in the rain, make Kool-Aid popsicles, mix up snow ice cream, and finger paint both at and on the kitchen table. As they got older, we would sing silly songs in the carpool lines, spend the day at the water park, and once in awhile, walk to school. Most of all, we laughed and hugged and said a million "I love you"s. On top of our scheduled craziness, there were kids, the ones from the neighborhood as well as my own, constantly running in and out of the house, squealing and raiding the pantry. Someone was always staying for dinner or doing homework in our living room. Life and it's day-to-day activities was crazy, busy, and fun, and were what made the days magical and worth living.

So yes, my sweet family, you could have proven your case. I looked frail and disabled, and most things still required tremendous effort on my part. I would often overexert myself and would be sore the next day. My plate was full and I was constantly doing something or going somewhere. The events of any given day would have probably been all the evidence you would have needed to convict me of overdoing it. But that same evidence was also proof of something else; it confirmed that I had made it, that I had truly survived, not just physically, but mentally, emotionally, and spiritually as well. I was living as I would have had tragedy not come into our lives. And that meant that I had reached my goal.

Mom, I realize that I was wasting my time worrying about you worrying. You would have done so no matter what I did. You're a mom; it's what you do. I just made it easier for you to do your job. But better that you were concerned with me being too active than you being worried because I had withdrawn and had closed the world out. At least my choices let you know that I had reasons to get out of bed in the morning, to not mind the effort it took to overcome the obstacles during the day, and to go to sleep each night with a smile on my face and gratitude in my heart. I was where I was supposed to be, doing what I was called to do. It could have been easier, but if those storms had passed me by, so too might have the magical moments, the lessons learned, the chances to make a difference, the fun, and the joy. So to my family I will say "Thank you for appeasing me." And to my husband and to God, I need to say, "Thank you for today and for the choices that I had in how to live it."

18

The Understanding

*"The higher up the mountain we go
the deeper the valleys will look,
but the better we will understand their terrain."
- Christi Kasha*

    Yes, there are all kinds of storms out there and countless forms of adversity that we will face. The best way for us to survive physically, mentally, and emotionally is to be prepared for them. We can't stop life from happening, but being able to recognize and understand what we are dealing with helps us to chart the course that is best for us.
    Many of life's storms are the kind that will roll in with the morning fog and will just as quickly roll out again. Others look as if they stretch past the horizon into forever, their intensity only building as they hover overhead. There are the storms that catch us by surprise in the middle of what we thought was going to be a peaceful and dream-filled night. And then there are those that fill us with fear and dread as we watch them

blowing in, moving closer and closer towards us. The agony of helpless waiting often causes more despair than the threatening elements themselves.

Your life may have been hit by a storm of adversity many years ago. Though you survived, the impact may have left you so battered and bruised that you scarcely notice the blue skies overhead today. Or perhaps the storm you now find yourself facing and having to fight your way through is as fresh as a new morning. Still reeling from the shock, you struggle to grasp what is happening. "This isn't how it is supposed to be!" and "What am I going to do?" you silently scream inside. If the winds would only break for a moment, you might have time to catch your breath. Then, maybe, you could take stock of the situation and figure out what to do next. But for now, your only hope seems to be to simply hang on the best you can and pray that the next wave won't be the one that knocks you overboard.

Some of the harshest storms are those that we misjudge. We might assume that the difficulty will pass quickly, only to find ourselves dealing with the pain and hardship over and over again. Or perhaps the adversity does disappear, but circles back around to hit us again. We thought we'd escaped the hold it had on us, and then, wham! While our previous encounters with this storm may have shown us what kind of threat it poses and taught us the best ways to handle it, the fact that we put our guard down, thinking we were safe, only to discover that the danger is still there, can cause more injury than the first encounter did.

The term "when the past comes back to bite you" would apply here. Then there are the periods in many of our lives when it feels like we have so many storms going on at once that it's hard to think about and keep track of them, much less know how to categorize and make plans for each one. In times like these, it often seems that the course to best get around one storm puts us directly in the path of another. It can appear that there's no route that will allow us to escape adversity, and we are forced to pick a storm to go through.

The dictionary's first definition for the word "storm" starts off: "A disturbance of the normal conditions of the atmosphere, manifesting itself with winds of unusual force or direction..." That pretty much covers it, does it not? When difficulty hits, what often throws us the most is that our normal circumstances change. Our circumstances don't have to be ideal or how we want our lives to stay forever for change to affect us. These less-than-perfect conditions of ours represent to us "normal" and we know what to expect from them. That predictability gives us comfort and security.

It's interesting that the definition says nothing about the size of the disturbance, only that it shows itself through a different force or direction. So if there is something "minor" that is going on in your life, don't beat yourself up over how strongly it's affecting you. Many times I have felt much more anger, sadness, and even depression over smaller trials than over the catastrophic events of my life. My feelings and reactions weren't based on how big the problem really was, but on how much the adversity changed my normal way of doing or thinking about things.

Then we come to the word "adversity." What a word! It is defined as "an adverse or unfortunate event or circumstances marked by misfortune, calamity or distress." To put it in terms that most of us can better relate to, adversity is when life slaps you in the face. Sometimes it stems from things out of our control. Sometimes we bring it upon ourselves. We may see it coming or it may catch us completely by surprise. But however it hits us, the sting still burns and the impact can leave us reeling for weeks, months, and even years afterwards.

For some of us, the word "adversity" causes thoughts of life-changing, traumatic events to rush to our minds. It sounds almost too nice to define the suffering and horror that we have had to endure. Illnesses, accidents, losing loved ones, abuse, betrayal, family breakups, extreme financial circumstances, and the consequences of bad decisions have brought us to our knees and have sometimes caused us to question our very existence. For others, it may be the daily struggles and disappointments that we associate with adversity. Physical challenges, financial worries, time conflicts, relationship problems, our own insecurities, and not knowing what decision to make or what action we should take can all push us to our limits. These things that we deal with constantly can cause us emotional, mental, and even physical pain. And it can be the kind of pain that leaves us hoping and praying to just make it through the present day.

Perhaps adversity represents to you, like it does to me, a combination of traumatic events and the daily battles that we have to fight. The reality and heaviness of one thing piled on top of another can leave us asking, "When will it end?" "Isn't enough enough?" and "Why me?" In many ways, we are the only ones who can answer these questions, and the answers will come from the way we decide to handle the storms and how we allow them to influence our journey.

Life holds adversity in one sense or another for all of us. But the good news is that adversity can hold life- if we know how to paddle through the storms to discover the joy.

19

The Paddles

"Life isn't a board game where how far we go is determined by a roll of the dice. It's more of a mathematical equation where distance equals dreams times effort."
- Christi Kasha

When dealing with true adversity, you might as well go ahead and take down the sails and pull out the paddles. Sailing might seem easier, but in the middle of a storm, it can be dangerous. Turbulent waters and unpredictable winds can cause you to lose control and end up far from your destination. You can choose to allow life's gusts and currents to take you where they may or you can decide -today- that your destiny and the outcome of your circumstances, no matter how discouraging and bleak they may seem, are up to you. If more control over your journey is what you want, then you should be prepared. There is no magic fix, no rescue chopper on the way, no perfect answer. It can take a lot of effort and tons of emotional, mental, and sometimes, as in my case, physical energy to paddle through a storm. And the course that you originally charted for your journey may not be the one that you end up needing to take.

THE PADDLES

Have you made your decision? Are you ready to do what it takes? If you aren't sure, that's okay. What that's telling you is that in some way you are comfortable where you are. The goal is to find joy in your journey, so if you have that, keep going! When or if you need a change, this book will be here for you. And whether you do or you don't need it, I wish for you contentment, happiness, blessings, and magical moments.

However, if you want to get out from under dark clouds and feel the sunshine, if you desire to live in the magic of life, if you are sitting there saying, "I don't care what I have to do, I'm ready for a change," then let's go! We are going to pull out the paddles that we can use to rescue ourselves from life's storms.

They have been there in your boat the whole time, but sometimes in the darkness and confusion that adversity can cause, it can be hard for us to locate them. It can also seem contradictory and strange to be getting these particular paddles out during a storm. They are the ones that we normally think of using on bright, sunny days, moonlit nights, and calm, peaceful voyages. But taking advantage of the power and magic they posses may be what will make all the difference in when and how we overcome our troubles. And by using them, when those dark clouds overhead finally do give way to the sun, you just might find yourself sitting in your boat with a smile on your face, enjoying the feel of the water's movement beneath you. You may even surprise yourself by looking upward and whispering, "Thank you for today and for this place that it has brought me to. It's beautiful here!"

Through necessity, my survival instincts, or perhaps, just plain old stubbornness, I managed to find these paddles. Using them is how I have been able to survive my personal tragedies. You have the same ones in your boat as I do, and you can use them anytime you need help overcoming a difficult situation. I will share with you how theses paddles have helped me and offer my recommendations for using them, but I should caution you that you will have to discover for yourself, sometimes by trial and error, sometimes by intuition or divine inspiration, and sometimes by pure luck, just how their power will best benefit you. Simply keep in mind that as long as you are making headway and as long as you find yourself smiling more than crying, laughing more than worrying, and feeling thankful more than resentful, you're doing it right and it's working.

So come on! There is a lot of joy on our journeys just waiting to be discovered. If you wait and you're lucky, it might come to you, but if you pull out these paddles, you can go find it. And I know where the sun is shining!

20

The First and the Ugliest Paddle

"Live with no excuses and love with no regrets."
- Montel

Let's get this over with. Of all of the paddles that I want to tell you about, this one is the least fun to handle and the ugliest to look at. But it is also the most important one to start with because we won't be able to use any of the other paddles correctly if we don't pick this one up first. So go ahead and grab hold of the Paddle of Awareness. You'll need it to come to an honest understanding of what you are going through, to take stock of your situation, and to help you find the sun.

But before you start rowing full speed ahead, let's make sure that you have given yourself time and permission to deal with the shock of what has happened or is happening to you. It's important to do this because it's part of the grieving process. Dr. Primo, whom I saw for my bi-optic glasses, explained to me that grief does not only occur with death. We can experience it with any kind of loss. For me, it was the loss of my eyesight and then the loss of my mobility and health. For you, it could be another type of health issue, the loss of a job, the breakup of your or your parents' marriage, the loss of your home, or a child moving away. The shock over your situation might manifest itself in the form of denial. "This can't be happening!" you want to scream. "It will pass," "It's not really that bad," "Someone must have made a mistake," and "She's coming back," are the types of normal things that we say to ourselves and to others when we are in shock or in denial. From those feelings we then need to move to the next stages of grief, which are anger, then attempting to make the situation better by bargaining, usually with God, and after that, depression. Often all of these stages need to be experienced before we can move forward. The amount of time it takes to do this will vary from individual to individual and from situation to situation. But after awhile we need to proceed to the final stage: acceptance. In order to do that, you are going to have to pick up that ugly Paddle of Awareness, stick it in the water, and come to understand your storm as much as possible.

To start the process, you need to have a clear picture of what you are facing. A good way to do this is by asking yourself questions. First, you need to determine how severe the problem really is. Use categories like meteorologists do to get started. "Is this a category four or a category eight storm?" Next look at the nature and the source of the problem by using general categories to help define it, such as "It's physical," "It's emotional," "I'm worried about money." Even saying honestly, "I don't know what's wrong. I just feel so frustrated (sad, angry, depressed, scared)," is a form of awareness. Then go on to judge the amount of control you did or didn't have over the situation by asking, "Was this something I saw coming or did it take me completely by surprise?" "Could I have done anything to prevent this?" "Does it seem like this is going to pass quickly, last for a while, or is it here to stay?"

After that tackle figuring out where this storm started. "Is this something internal or did external situations cause it?" It might be a combination of the two. Your company shutting down is no reflection on you personally, but it may bring up old feelings of failure and uncertainty. Are the present circumstances of your life causing this or are you trying to come to terms with issues from your past? Again, keep in mind that one can lead to the other. What kinds of changes will this mean for you and how do you think those changes will impact your day-to-day living? Then, most importantly, ask yourself how you feel. Are you sad, mad, scared, confused, hopeless, or resentful? Be honest, be realistic, and understand that there isn't a "right answer" to these questions. They are your feelings! And because feelings can change in a split second, you might bounce back and forth between different ones or feel nothing one moment and all of them the next. You can share your emotions or keep them private. But just remember, that while this may be painful to think about, ignoring your feelings won't move you forward. We have to understand the dark clouds overhead to know how to handle them.

Once you have defined and have a clear picture of your storm, you will be more equipped to decide what action to take. Will this storm pass if you just wait it out or are you going to have to fight through it? Does it require action or patience? Will it be temporary or is it here to stay? It might be a situation where certain parts can be resolved and others you are stuck with. With my encephalitis, there was no way to know what would improve and what wouldn't. Some of my struggles required action, while some needed time to get better. With my eyesight, the threat of a disease or a tumor passed, but I was left coping with a disability that no action could fix. However, there were things that I could do to reduce its impact.

You need to also ask yourself if you can deal with this issue by yourself or do you really need some help and/or support. Some types of boats navigate better with one person at the wheel. Others are built for a crew. For me, this one is easy to answer, but tough to accept. Some things I need help with, but don't want. With other things I want help, but it either isn't what is best for me or it isn't available. When I need help reading something, I'll holler out to Ansley and Faith, "I need some eyes," but I wish so badly that I didn't have to bother them and that I could just do it myself. With my limp and with my arm's limited motion, I would happily accept someone's help in fixing it. But it's just not available.

The type and the amount of assistance that we want and need can depend on our personality. I am more of a private person and talking about what I'm feeling sometimes makes me feel even more frustrated and down. I do better working through it on my own, at least to a certain point. Other people heal and cope better by sharing and discussing what they are going through. My brother, Scott, and his wife, Denise, lost three precious babies during pregnancy through two miscarriages and a stillbirth. They found that support groups with other parents who had experienced similar tragedies helped them understand and better deal with their pain. I thank God that they had somewhere to turn for the support they needed during their storm. But I had to be aware of my own needs and trust myself enough to turn down suggestions for me to attend support groups for my vision, my illness, and for a miscarriage that I had. It was important that I understood it was okay if I didn't handle my adversity the same way they handled theirs.

Where we should turn and how much outside support we need can also depend on the amount of information and experience we ourselves have and on how much support our close family and friends can offer. Sometimes the people we're the closest to can share and show their love for us, but don't know how or aren't able to give us the kind of help and support that we need. In such cases, draw strength from and lean on their love, but find other sources to rely on for guidance and the appropriate help.

We do, however, need to be very honest with ourselves about all of our answers because honesty leads to awareness and awareness moves us forward. If I had said that support groups were not what I needed as a way of avoiding talking about my situation or if my brother and sister-in-law went to groups to escape intimately dealing with their own pain, neither of us would have been doing the right thing. Using this paddle includes understanding and being upfront with yourself about why decisions are being made.

Awareness also means not making a mountain out of a molehill, but not sticking your head in the sand either. Neither will help you in the long run. Ignoring a problem often makes it worse and lets us know that we are stuck back in the denial stage. Perhaps it's time for you to lift your head up and face the threatening clouds. They might not be as bad as you think. And you just might discover something wonderful that's waiting for you with the next step.

Or are you coping by acting as though your life is in danger when really the water is only a little choppy? It can be scary to think that the action we believe we should take won't be good enough or won't make a significant difference. So you figure that making no decision will be better than making the wrong one. Therefore, you act as though circumstances are out of your control and are just too horrible to do anything about. This strategy can seem safe because you are not putting

THE FIRST AND UGLIEST PADDLE

as much on the line and no one can blame you for the outcome. But the problem is you'd better take a liking to those storm clouds above you because they might be there for awhile. You see, in exchange for no risk, you just gave up your control. Life requires movement, and movement requires action. The only question is who decides what action takes place, someone or something else, or you? It takes a lot of awareness to be able to recognize that you are using this strategy. If you realize that you are doing this, congratulate yourself first! You just took a big leap forward! Then stick your Paddle of Awareness in the water and take some action to propel yourself even farther. You don't have to go around a mountain, just paddle over the molehill.

The Awareness Paddle isn't the easiest to handle. In fact, it can get awfully heavy. And just as soon as you figure out how to work it, your circumstances may change, the tide may reverse directions, the clouds may shift, and you will need to start all over again. But using it gives us the power to make things better for ourselves and to keep control of our journey. Just be realistic about what you are dealing with. A heavy flood is very different from a tornado. While they can both be dangerous, the actions we need to take to protect ourselves are vastly different.

Awareness can be difficult, but keep this paddle close by even when it gets in the way. It may not be fun to look at or to hold, but it will set us off on the right course.

21

The Paddle of Hope

*"Don't judge each day by the harvest you reap,
but by the seeds you plant."
- Robert Louis Stevenson*

Pick up the Paddle of Hope next and discover the power that it will give you.

Hope is what keeps us going when there doesn't seem to be a reason to continue. It convinces us to keep fighting even when the fight appears to be futile. When today was horrible, hope whispers to us that there is always tomorrow. It is our light at the end of the tunnel. To those of us who have learned to depend on hope, it is no surprise that the rainbow is used to symbolize it. They both remind us that after a storm the sun will still shine and something beautiful and seemingly magical can come from even the heaviest of downpours.

Sometimes knowing in advance all that it's going to take for us to get through a crisis can be too much to comprehend and handle at once, especially when we are already in a fragile or weakened state. The Paddle of Hope is the tool we can use to break down what lies ahead of us on our journey into legs that don't seem impossible to navigate. If we pick a point on the horizon that is easily visible and that we can focus on, we can then use this paddle to get us there. That one point is all that we have to think about, work towards, and believe that we can attain. Once we reach it, we can pick a new spot on the next horizon to focus on and start paddling towards, and from there, one on the next horizon, and then again on the next. Eventually we will find that by using hope, we have found our way to blue skies where we sit mesmerized by the rainbow.

Looking back, there have been countless times in my life, be it for just a moment, an hour, a day, or an extended period, when I am certain that I would not have made it through a storm had I not used this strategy. I wasn't aware that I was doing it at the time, but that is exactly what was taking place. Ten years ago I was lying in hospital bed with a doctor telling us that it would probably take about two years for me to completely recover from the encephalitis. "Oh, I don't think so!" I remember silently countering. "I'll give it one year tops!" I had just picked up the Paddle of Hope and was headed towards my horizon.

Somehow our survival instincts know how much we can mentally and emotionally handle. Right then, the thought of spending two years in pain, sick, and incapacitated was more than I could bear. I truly believe that if I had known then that ten years down the road I would still be suffering from the effects of that illness, I would have given up, period. Thankfully, I didn't know it, nor did I need to. I just needed to use hope to get me to the farthest point that I could see from where I was. At that moment, my horizon was one year away; that hope would let me reach. So I started paddling towards it with everything I had.

If thinking about the future doesn't make you feel better, then you are probably using this paddle incorrectly. You may be looking at and worrying over points that are too far away from where you are with your current circumstances. Your survival instincts won't let you focus that far off. Try picking another point and make another goal. Use the "back it up plan" if needed to find the horizon that feels right and that you can believe in. Here's how it works: whatever you are going through, think about how you want it to turn out and where you want to be in, say, a year from now. Does that thought make you feel good or do you find yourself grimacing at it? If the answer is that it gives you hope and makes you feel energized and happy, then you are focusing exactly where you should be, so get to paddling. However, if thinking about reaching that point next year is frustrating, discouraging, or makes you feel sad, depressed or angry, back it up. You can do this in two ways, either lower your expectations of where you want to be or reduce the amount of time that you plan on taking to reach your destination. For example, let's say that you are struggling with finances and you want to pay off a credit card that has a $5,000 balance on it. If thinking of having it paid off by this time next year doesn't make you smile and instead makes you feel tense, then back up your plan. How do you feel thinking of having that credit card paid off in six months instead of twelve? Does thinking of paying half of the $5,000 seem more hopeful? Continue playing with scenarios until you feel that you can and will get there.

Or it could be that you have lost someone you love deeply. You want so badly to move on, but it just seems that you are stuck in your sadness and depression, or maybe as in the case of a breakup, confusion and anger are what you're wrestling with. Nothing seems to help. Take a look at where you're expecting this to end up. If the thought of ever being happy again seems completely out of reach, back it up. If you are focusing on getting back what you have lost and you really know that either it can't or it shouldn't happen, back it up. Find something more realistic to think about.

Many years ago I was in a bad marriage that lasted under a year. As it drew to an end, I knew that I needed confirmation that life would one day be good again. At that moment I didn't need to worry about my distant future, lost plans, or even what I was going to do next. I just needed to know that my misery was a temporary problem and that I would survive this. So I called Marshall, one of my best and oldest friends. We had been high school and college sweethearts and I trusted him completely. "Hey, Marsh."

"Christi! What are you doing?"

"I'm calling to see what you're doing tonight." It was a Saturday night, odds were he had plans.

"I'm getting ready to go out with some friends. Why?"

"You taking a date?" I boldly asked.

"Nope. It's mostly just the guys." The guys were a good bunch.

"I need to get out of here and do something fun. I'll explain later. Can I join you? I promise not to cramp your style."

"We're getting ready to leave. How soon can you be here?"

"I can walk out the door right now."

"Come on!"

The paddle worked and hanging out with Marshall gave me the hope I needed. The evening was spent eating, drinking, dancing, and laughing. In the middle of one of the most disappointing times in my life, I found that I could still have fun.

You'll notice that I didn't say that it was one of the saddest times in my life. There comes a point in certain types of adversity when relief can replace previous emotions, proof that we are moving forward. Also notice that I called someone whom I knew could make me smile and wouldn't take advantage of me or my vulnerability. I needed to spend time with somebody who would boost my hope for things to get better, not make me feel worse about men in general or myself. Making bold, yet smart, decisions also shows progress and gives us more control.

Thank you, Marshall, for the hope, the fun, the magical moments, and the love! If you ever need me, I'm here. And I know, I know, I still owe you a couple of drinks.

I reached my horizon and found that my misery wasn't permanent. My hope had been renewed and so I picked another point to shoot for. One thing at a time is how I got through that storm.

Three months later, it was a beautiful sunny day when I went to a Braves baseball game with my friend, Dawn, who had been my maid of honor, her boyfriend, and some other friends of theirs. After the game, we grabbed a bite to eat and then went back to their apartment. Giving hugs and saying goodbye, I headed out. Dawn's boyfriend's brother walked me to my car. As we stood there laughing about the day's events, he asked me out for the next weekend. I said yes. His name was Terry. Hope had quickly taken me a long way from where I had been.

So pick up your paddle and see what's waiting just over the horizon. Start with a point that you can reach tomorrow. It can be making a phone call, asking someone to go to lunch to talk, setting an appointment, sending just one email, making a list, taking a short walk, cleaning out a drawer, or doing ten sit-ups. Whatever it is, it's okay to start with that. Trying to do too much will backfire on you. Later you can do more. But for now, just take some action, any action. It's a great way to prove to yourself that you have control over your life and that this storm doesn't have to last forever.

Action will also boost your hope because the magic of this paddle is that it gains power each time it is used. Make it to your first horizon and your next goal will seem even more attainable. I had said that I would be fully recovered from my illness in one year at the most. At the end of that period, I was better, but I still had a long, long way to go. Yet hope from the past year transferred easily to the next year and had given me a new perspective. Twelve months didn't seem as far away as it had. "Well, the doctor did say that it would probably take two years." I could then accept his words. "One more year of this is not that long. And if it takes even longer than that, oh well, it will be okay. I can do it."

A decade has passed and I am nowhere near back to normal, well, my old "normal" that is. But you never know how things will go this year or the next or the next. I haven't put the Paddle of Hope down yet, so we'll see.

The flip side of this advice is that while you don't want to set your sights on something that ends up making you feel discouraged, the mundane things that we need to do to overcome the adversity often don't spark our hope and don't seem worth the effort. If you struggle with this, let me share my strategy. I trick myself into doing those things by hoping for something bigger than the task at hand. You can transform what you need to do into something that is worth your effort, something that you can get excited about and that has emotional strings attached to it.

For me, walking any distance is usually challenging, to say the least. It can be very hard and even painful depending on everything from my recent activities to the surface that I'm walking on. Not long ago I told my friend, Gale, that based on the effort I have to put forth, my walk around the circle in our neighborhood would probably equate to a 5K race for many people. Jokingly, I said that I wanted a t-shirt or a medal. She, who has run a half marathon, is supposed to be getting me one. Because it is both physically and emotionally difficult for me, I have to talk myself into taking a stroll. Yes, I need the exercise and I like being outside, but it can be hard to make myself do it. So I tie it into things that are more meaningful or exciting and that I have a stronger desire to attain. Then it's worth the effort.

We had planned a family vacation to the southwestern United States, visiting the Grand Canyon and eight other National Parks, Mexico, and Las Vegas. Terry and I had taken this trip before we had kids, so I knew how much walking we were talking about. I could not bear the thought of ruining this vacation for my girls or letting my physical limitations hold us back. So, boom! I had found a way to change my negative view of walking into something meaningful. Suddenly hope for a vacation that we would always treasure became my driving force. Walking around the neighborhood was no longer exercise, it was training for an important event. The vacation was wonderful! There were times that it was tough, but I held my own.

After that was over, I needed to be motivated by the hope of doing something else meaningful. I chose the Peachtree Road Race, a 10K run that's held in downtown Atlanta every Fourth of July. My brothers, my dad, and several friends have the prestigious t-shirts that finishers get. I didn't have one, but I would.

I planned out my training schedule, starting slow by jogging only a tenth of a mile and building on that each week. Family members thought that either brain damage had finally shown up or that I really was in denial over my condition. "Why in the world would the idea of running a 10K race even enter into your head when you have trouble walking a mile?" they wondered with worry. Although I'm not sure they ever understood it, they had answered their own question. It was because trying to walk a mile was so depressing. But training for a race is supposed to be hard, and therefore, the difficulty was expected. And because I'd be working towards something that I had dreamed of doing, it would make me feel encouraged versus discouraged. Not to mention that training for a 6.2 mile run would mean that I'd have to be able to walk a mile easily. Using the power in the Paddle of Hope to reach what was worth my effort would cause me to pay little attention to what depressed me as I passed right by it.

Is there something that you need to aim higher for in order to make the first step exciting enough to take? To do this, focus on something that already matters to you or create something to dream about. If you are trying to pay off a credit card, do it so that you can use it to take your dream vacation. Go ahead, plan the vacation. Go on that diet to get ready for your Caribbean cruise. If you are struggling in a certain class, study as if the dean of the college you really want to go is going to be your substitute teacher. If you don't like your job, work as though you are in training for your promotion. Do you need to improve your health? See yourself dancing at your child's or grandchild's wedding. You do want to be around for it, right?. Are you worried about finding Mr. Right? Then go on dates as if you're just having fun until he crosses your path and falls madly in love with you at first sight. What a magnificent story you'll have about how you met! And who knows? The guy sitting across from you might have just fallen. When all else fails, just pretend that you're going through your storms so that you can write a book to help other people get through theirs. Try it. It works!

I still don't own a Peachtree Road Race t-shirt. Life's currents caused me to have to change my direction and focus. Does it matter? Well, yes and no. No, because hope was used to get me farther than I had been. I made progress and I had fun doing so! It might still not be easy, but I can walk a mile today and will sometimes do so just for the fun of the challenge. On the other hand, yes, it does matter, but not in a negative sense. Not reaching my goal means that I can still use it as a motivator. Someone make sure those officials at the t-shirt table know that I'm going to want a large.

What we come down to is that there is a fine line between setting your sights on something so far away that you get discouraged and focusing on something that is important enough to make it worth the effort that's needed. Just where that line is drawn is something that you will have to figure out for yourself with each individual storm that comes your way.

The key is to choose a horizon that makes you feel energized, positive, and happy. Using the Paddle of Hope should bring about even more hope. It should make you feel as though the next marker is within your reach. When used correctly, this amazing paddle has the power to transform your thoughts and desires into actions and reality. Just remember this- hope isn't the finish line, hope is what gets us out of the gate.

22

The Paddle of Fear

*"Fear is just a magnifying glass held over
what matters the most to us."*
- Christi Kasha

There is a paddle that would seem hope's counterpart. It's the Paddle of Fear. That's right, fear. We can use this strange, unnerving emotion to lessen the hold that adversity has on us. While hope can convince us that things will get better and that our lives will turn out as we want, fear of what might happen if things don't go our way can be an awfully powerful force to contend with.

Read the following scenario, then I am going to ask you to close your eyes for a moment and let it play out in your head. Two canoes are anchored at the same dock. In the first, the rower is told secretly that on a buoy floating in the distance there is a million dollars in cash. If he gets there first, it's his. He tries to hide the smile that comes to his face. The look in his eyes is a mixture of excitement and determination. In the other canoe, the rower is handed a note to read silently. It states that his wife and children are being held hostage. The price for their freedom is the million dollars that is on the buoy. He must get there first to claim it. The look that flashes across his face can neither be hidden nor described. Both boats are untied and at the same time the men are told, "Ready, set, go!" Close your eyes now and envision the race. Open them when you have a winner. Go.

Is your heart pounding? Thank God that this is only a hypothetical situation I made up to help us understand the kind of power that fear possesses. I would venture to guess that you couldn't help but see in your mind stark differences in the way the two men would row those canoes and in their demeanors while doing so. In reality, there are many other non-emotional factors that would determine who would actually reach the million dollars first, but in my mind the man whose family is being held hostage is who I am rooting for and he will win every time. We can see how fear can cause us to fight like nothing else and to do things that we wouldn't normally think of doing, even when the odds are against us. And sometimes that is just exactly what we need.

Sitting on my sofa while I was recovering from my illness, my body burning and aching, I sure didn't feel like doing much of anything. When I did force myself to get up, I spent as much time tripping, stumbling, falling, and catching my breath as I did actually walking. I was pathetic and a husband's nightmare. But there was something much more powerful going on than the physical hardships.

There was fear, not the fear of falling and getting hurt and not the fear of the pain that often accompanied even the simplest of movements. It was the fear of what would happen if I didn't risk the falls, if I didn't make my muscles move, or if I let the pain decide what I was capable of doing. I was terrified of what it would do to my little girl if I didn't pick her up, give her a bath, walk her to the playground, or take her to storytime at the library. The thought of the regrets that I would have if I let the pain cause me to miss out on all of those special moments with my newborn baby scared me as much as anything. And there was the fear of letting opportunities to do the things I was passionate about pass me by and not getting another chance. Those were the fears that scared me into action and gave me cause to keep fighting when the waters were the roughest.

If you are feeling stuck under the storm clouds or if you see them headed your way, maybe it's time to take out the Paddle of Fear. It might be just what you need to prompt you to fight and to propel you into action. Fear is a part of our survival instincts for a reason and it can cause us to row in a manner that no type of excitement ever can, so grab hold of this emotion and figure out how to use it to your advantage.

This may seem strange. We are, after all, told to look on the bright side, to think positive, to keep the faith. I am as firm of a believer in that kind of thinking as you will probably ever meet, partially due to my nature and partially due to my life experiences. But there are times when we need something to kick us in the pants and get us going. Most of us have also been taught that if something frightens us, we should face those fears head on and overcome them. I agree with that philosophy as well and have tried to teach it to my children. But before you run those fears off, see if you can use them. Often we can learn more about ourselves from our enemies than from our friends. So it is with our fears and our joys.

If you are wondering how to even begin to get something positive and uplifting from that which you are afraid of, start by asking yourself two questions. First, what about this storm scares you the most? And second, what is the worst possible outcome that could come from it? Your answers will show what your priorities are and what you will work the hardest for.

For me, there was more than just one answer to that first question, and yet, all of my answers really came back around to the same point. My greatest fear was that what I was going through would change me in a negative way. I didn't want my problems to make me an unhappy person who didn't enjoy life or whose thoughts were always focused on the negative side of things. I wanted to be a certain type of mother to my children and I didn't want to not see the beauty in the world around me. I've known people who have been through horrible tragedies, and although they survived, the tragedies still have the upper hand because it is those horrible events that define them and their lives. No thank you! That was, and still is, one of my fears.

What about for you? No matter how simple or complex your answer is, what does it really point to? Does your greatest fear with this storm involve the impact that it could have on your emotional well-being, your physical health, financial affairs, the relationships in your life, family, career, your passion, or your dreams for the future? Whatever it is, that is your hot button. That is the thing that you are the most likely to do what you have to do to defend and protect. Keep it fresh in your mind because once you have identified the fear, you can think through what the worst possible outcome or outcomes of this adversity might be. Avoidance of that possible result can motivate you to overcome countless obstacles.

I didn't have one simple answer for the second question either- what the worst possible outcome might be. It was a combination of the unbearable thought of what if I didn't get any better and the even harder to bear thought that my kids might not enjoy their childhood or feel close to me. Added to that, was the idea that I might look back with regrets of not what I had done, but of what I had chosen not to do. Knowing and being aware of those things, even if I wasn't consciously thinking them, is what got my butt off the sofa, insisted that I play even when it could be painful, gave me reasons to do the daily stuff from cooking to cleaning, made transporting kids to and from activities that much more special, and made me feel stronger about volunteering. Yes, the Paddle of Fear can give us the strength to get far away from the storm clouds and the insight to understand why it's worth our effort.

But be aware that the Paddle of Fear can be one of the more tricky paddles to manage. While fear can cause us to fight battles that we wouldn't normally take on, it can also become tempting and easy to use as an excuse for making decisions that aren't really in our best interest.

So how can we tell if we are using fear productively or unproductively? An easy way to check yourself is to see which of the two following statements most closely resembles what you say when you are making a decision. Do your thoughts start off with some variation of "I'm scared to..." or is your focus more on "I'm scared not to..."? If you answer, "I'm scared to...," it could very well be a signal that you are letting fear hold you back from something you want or need to do. All of the following statements seem to express hesitancy or avoidance: "I'm scared to try it in case it doesn't work." "I'm scared to go for it." "I'm scared of how she'll respond." "I'm scared that I'll get hurt." "I'm scared that I'll look stupid." In none of these is fear used as a motivator and is stopping productivity. On the contrary, statements such as: "I'm scared not to give it a shot." "I'm scared that I'll never forgive myself if I don't try." "I'm scared not to tell him how I feel." "I'm scared that not doing so will make me feel worse," show that fear is driving you to do something that doesn't seem easy.

Please understand that I am m in no way

suggesting or advocating that you ignore fear when it comes to doing something that could be dangerous to your physical, emotional, or mental well-being. Again, fear is part of our survival instincts and there's a good reason for that; it's called keeping us safe. Saying, "I'm scared not to try drugs with my friends because they won't want to be with me," is by no means what I'm talking about. I am saying that fear can sometimes be used to help you overcome your adversity, but never should it bring more into your life. Trust your instincts and remember that a friend who asks you to do something that doesn't feel right to you or that you wouldn't be proud of anyone and everyone knowing about, isn't your friend. Don't forget that friends love and lift.

Not too long ago, Terry, the girls, and I were at a restaurant that had karaoke going. Faith is a naturally gifted singer and has a beautiful voice. She was excited about having a chance to perform for an audience. When I told her to come with me to put her name on the list and pick out a song, she froze. I quickly realized that she was scared. While having sung in quite a few productions, she had never performed solo.

"Come on, Faith," Ansley encouraged, "I'll sing if you will!"

There was no hesitation on Ansley's part. She has been singing in front of people since the age of three when she earned her first dollar at a restaurant by joining the house band in singing every word of Lee Greenwood's "God Bless the USA." A few years back, she was brave enough to take on singing the National Anthem at a school event in front of all her peers and their parents. She was fantastic and I was in tears.

But it was obvious that Faith was still fighting with herself over her fears. "I know you'll do great if you want to sing, but you certainly don't have to," I told her.

"I don't know. I really want to. I'm just scared, Mommy."

"I know you are, Precious." I stroked her long, silky, brown hair. "I can't tell you what to do on this one, but I do need you to decide soon because we can't stay here all night."

"I don't know what to do!" She was close to tears and angry at herself.

"Well, Faith, let me ask you something. Are you going to be more disappointed if you get up there and mess up or if we leave here and you didn't sing?"

After thinking for a few seconds, she grinned. Fifteen minutes later the DJ announced to the audience, "I believe that we might be looking at a future American Idol," after Faith had finished her solo singing debut. Ansley kept her promise and received a rousing ovation from the audience.

Understanding and evaluating her fears helped my little girl make the decision that was right for her. In the end, you are the only one who can do that for your situation. Only you can know for sure if fear is being used to get out of the storm or if it's keeping you rowing in circles. If the answer isn't what it should be, ask yourself some questions, find the answers, change what you are saying to yourself, and start rowing in a direction where the joy that is waiting for you can be discovered.

23

The Paddle of Confidence

"The biggest influence on how others see you is how you see yourself."
- Christi Kasha

All right, I see it. And, yes, it looks heavy to me too. It's the Paddle of Confidence. Most of us would never believe that we have the strength to even pick it up, much less use it during times of adversity. For the large majority of people, confidence is hard to come by in the best of times. During life's storms, it becomes an even rarer commodity. That is when we are more likely to beat ourselves up by thinking things such as, "If I were really as good as I should be, I wouldn't be struggling with this problem," and "If only I had done the right thing, said the right thing, handled things differently, then I wouldn't be in this mess."

Having confidence in yourself may seem a far stretch from where you are now. I can relate; I live with this issue every day. High self-esteem has never been at the top of the list of my strong character traits, although I've learned over the years how to hide my insecurities pretty well and sometimes how to just ignore them.

In fact, I was getting frustrated with trying to write this chapter. The things that I want to share just wouldn't come out the way I wanted. I found myself stumbling from one thought to another. Finally giving up, I went to watch a television show with Terry. We were going to have some ice cream and I knew that if anything would help, it would be ice cream. My mind was still somewhat on this Confidence Paddle as the show began. Suddenly it hit me! No wonder I was having trouble giving recommendations for using this tool, it's the one that I struggle with the most. I'm still trying to figure it out for myself. However, while I might not have it down pat, I do know for sure just how important it really is, for even a little confidence in ourselves and in our abilities can be like wearing a life preserver. It gives you the security that you will come back up to the surface should you get pulled under. So I'll share with you what I have discovered and we will muddle through this one together.

First of all, I know that there is a little part of each of us that knows true confidence. Look at a little child and the confidence that he naturally has. "I can do it," he says matter-of-factly.

"I'm okay," she announces after falling while trying something new. Before she finishes the words, she is back up to try again.

"No, I'm not worried about looking silly," a child would scoff. "That's just part of learning how to do it right. Silly adults!"

We are all born with natural confidence, but that part of us can get pushed way down during the course of our lives, usually with the help of things both said and unsaid by the people close to us - parents, siblings, teachers, friends. And the older we get, the harder it can be to hear and believe what that part is telling us, especially when a storm is raging. But if we listen closely and openly enough, we can make out what our soul is whispering to us, and we'll see that the thoughts we have of "if only I had done things differently" and "I'm not good enough" shouldn't be any more of an issue now than they were when we were little children and messed up while trying something new.

We often judge ourselves as we look back at our past. But the problem with doing that is that hindsight isn't always 20/20. It can be easy to lose confidence while realizing how we could have done things differently, but we must keep in mind that one change usually leads to another. Had you made even one decision differently, it may have started a chain reaction and nothing would be the same. The end result may be far from what you would imagine. Perhaps you did make the best decisions after all.

As for feeling that you aren't good enough, think about all of the inspiring and motivational success stories that you've heard about people who came out of horrible circumstances, rose above an ugly past, defied the odds, and became someone that others admire and aspire to be like.

There isn't anything better about them than you or anyone else. Those people simply decided to take control and row themselves out of the storm. Somewhere along their journeys, they found the Paddle of Confidence and used it to build up their belief in themselves.

You can do the same. Talk to yourself, whether verbally, silently, or by writing things down, just as a supportive parent, teacher, or friend would, and point out to yourself how valuable you are, in big and little ways. See yourself as a child brave enough to attempt something and knowing in advance that falling is just part of the process. No, this isn't called being conceited or snotty, it's called self-esteem. Just like fear, whether it is good or bad depends on how we use it. If having confidence helps you get to a better place in your life emotionally, and that allows you to give more of yourself to others, then rest assured, it's a good thing. So start rowing!

Starting out, it can be extremely hard to believe in yourself and to have faith in the decisions you make, even the small, simple ones. This difficulty is easily heightened when other people around you aren't struggling, or when those you are the closest to, as was the case with my family, don't understand your decisions and worry about what you are doing. That's why it is so important to be able to believe in yourself, trust your instincts, and have confidence in your ability to see yourself through this storm. As sad and as harsh as it may sound, there are times in life when you might be all that you have.

The support and encouragement that I received from my parents growing up gave me the strength to get this paddle moving. The irony is that they were the ones who worried the most about me trying too much. It's called the pros and cons of family love. But there are some of you that did not have that support as a child, and today you may well be starting at square one. First, know that you are more than capable of boosting your self-confidence on your own. But if you would like a jump-start, ask a family member or a friend to tell you one strength or positive thing that you possess. You might be surprised at how other people see you.

A friend's comment about something she saw as a strength of mine is why I am writing this book. Gale asked me one day how I can stay so positive. She told me that it was surprising that I didn't mind being around her. She is a strong athlete and often talks about her love for running. At the time she made this comment, she was training for her half-marathon. "If I were in your shoes, it would be hard for me to be around other athletes. You were always athletic. It seems like it would make you think too much about the things you can't do now. But you don't let it stop you."

"There are things that I can't do?" I acted mockingly shocked and horrified as I limped over to the sofa.

What I was really thinking was, "Wow!" Somebody just took my disabilities and flipped them into assets. Talk about a confidence boost. Thanks, Gale!

If you are not in the kind of environment where you can ask someone close to you to tell you a strength you have, ask a co-worker or a person that you see on a regular basis. And if you really want the truth, just ask a child or a senior citizen. Don't be shy. Asking for what you need is a good way to prove that you can have faith in yourself. To make it easier, I'll give you an example of what you can say. Try this: "I'm so embarrassed to be doing this, but can I ask a quick favor of you? I'm reading this book about getting through tough times. Feeling better about yourself is one thing that's supposed to help. So the crazy author challenged me to ask someone that I know pretty well (or "that I don't know very well") if he (or "she") would tell me something positive he has noticed about me. I feel comfortable enough with you to ask if you would at least make up something to tell me." The point of phrasing it that way is even if you don't get your answer, you just gave that person a compliment by saying they make you feel comfortable. And you never know who needs a little boost before they can pick up their paddle. But most likely what this person, who isn't even close to you, says will surprise you. It could be that what you do like about yourself comes through more than you think or it may be that something you haven't even thought of, others see as being special.

Understanding that many things in our lives are really just a matter of perspective can make a difference in how you see yourself. If you are having a hard time doing what you need to do in order to escape your storm, the solution might be as simple as changing your view of yourself. Something my brother, Matt, said to me in the hospital has helped me over the past ten years with my self-esteem. At the time, it meant a lot to me, but I had no idea how many times I would replay his words in my head. He was with me one day when some sweet friend came to visit. After they left, Matt said to me in his astute, wiser than most, loving way, "Christi, when everyone is talking about all of the miracles that God has given you, please just remember that the greatest one is how He made you to begin with." I questioned what he meant by that. He explained that he felt that the main reason things had turned out so positively for me was because of the qualities and traits that I was born with. I seem to recall the words "stubborn" and "hard-headed" being used; he is my younger brother after all.

When I am feeling hopeless, down, or misunderstood, I'll say to myself, "Remember what Matt said. I already have what I need to make it through this." or "I can do this. I've got what it takes. That's just how I'm made." Looking at myself that way has helped me to not worry so much what others think about how I'm paddling my boat. "Well, that's the way I was born. How I'm handling this feels right to me and I need to trust that. Others might not understand because they're not made the same way, just as I probably wouldn't understand if the shoe was on the other foot," I remind myself.

You can build up your confidence by thinking about the strengths and qualities that you were born with. It's kind of fun. Ask yourself which of your unique gifts and attributes could play a role in a "miracle" taking place. I can answer that for you- all of them, when the situation presents a need. Think of how the person you are can help you overcome your adversity. Maybe it's your patience or your humor. How about your analytical ability or your gentle nature? Is it your flexibility, your musical talent, or your street savvy? And there's no telling where that combination of creativity and stubbornness can take you.

When we are in a tough situation, it is so easy to focus on the negative, especially when some of our characteristics were used in a negative manner and led us into the dark thunderheads. We can easily "if only..." ourselves to death. "If only I was more like this" and "If only I was less like that."

My advice- stop! You aren't like this and you are like that, so use it! Let the little child in you remind you it's okay to not be perfect. Then try saying to yourself, "I might not have (blank), but I do have (blank), and that could be the one thing that will see me through this. It might be what will make a miraculous difference in my life." You'll find a sweet warmth that comes from just thinking of yourself that way. Try it, go ahead, try it right now. Say those words to yourself, plugging one trait that you don't have and a special one that you do have into the blanks. It may feel weird to talk about yourself in a positive way. For way too many people, it just may be the first time you can recall being praised. To those people I say this,

"It's about time! You deserve the praise and the recognition! Just because someone hasn't said it, doesn't make it any less true!" Pull back out the Paddle of Fear if you need a boost, but give this a shot. You never know how far one single stroke with the Paddle of Confidence might take you.

I had, no, I have many reasons to not feel confident in myself and that make me need to reexamine my perspective. I'm constantly aware of how noticable one or more of my handicaps are and how strange I probably look at any given moment. Embarrassment is a part of every day life for me and there are so many things that I can't do or can't do "right." But somewhere along the way, I had to decide that if I was going to live the life that I wanted to live and if I wanted to be happy, then I was going to have to let go of what I couldn't do and focus on the things that I could do. Before I knew it, finding just enough confidence to attempt one thing, and it not killing me, gave me the confidence to do something else. When that wasn't a total flop, I gained a little more to try something else. Things haven't always gone perfectly, trust me, and I realize that people probably stare and whisper behind my back more than I want to know, but I have learned a lot, grown a lot, and laughed a lot.

Here is how to get this paddle going- focus on your strengths, pick something that is worth the risk to you, listen to that child's voice inside of you, and take some action. No matter what the outcome, you'll live through it, and that alone will boost your belief in yourself as I found out. Yes, this is certainly not the paddle that I am the most comfortable with, but I don't believe in asking of someone else what you yourself are not willing to do, so here are some examples that I'll share with embarrassment and use as reminders to myself in the "I can't do this, but I can do that" exercise:

I couldn't walk without a stagger or a limp, but I could easily talk to kids, and I loved making them laugh. So I would often go eat lunch with my daughters and their friends at school. Ansley and Faith knew to either come get me or to wave really big when they saw me come in. Otherwise it could take me forever to find them in the sea of faces, thanks to my blurry vision. I'll admit that I was self-conscious about struggling at the visitor sign-in and walking funny down the halls or through the cafeteria. But they always acted so appreciative when I came and I would leave with a smile on my face, so the quick moments of embarrassment seemed a small price to pay for the return I got for my efforts.

Then there's my singing voice. Let's just say that at church I "make a joyful noise to the Lord." Once Terry told me that I could join the praise team and either sing tenor or solo. Laughing at himself, he went on to explain, ten-or twelve miles away or so-low that no one could hear me. On another occasion, Matt asked me why no matter what I sing, it sounds like Kermit the Frog. So, fine, I might not be a gifted singer, but I do know how to get kids to sing their little hearts out and I know that adding sign language helps them remember the song and make it more fun while teaching them another language. So me and my Kermit tenor voice led the children's choir for several years. The memories I have from doing so will be with me forever!

Some other "positive focus" points for me are that while I might not have much physical endurance and can't work on the house or the yard like I once did, I can think up and organize fun, unique, at-home birthday parties that are easy, inexpensive, and will accommodate as many kids as want to come. I've heard on more than one occasion, "You're nuts!" from other parents and "Thank you, Mommy!" from my kids. I also now have a harder time physically cooking, but apparently my chocolate milkshakes "rock" and are needed during movie time when friends sleep over. It is emotionally hard for me to not able to easily read any book that I want to my kids. But I'm good at making up fun family activities and creative memory hints when studying for tests. We didn't have the money to support all of the charities that I wish we could have, but I had the inspiration and the drive to pursue and implement a community outreach program at the church. I sometimes yell when it's not needed and overreact to things that the girls do or forget to do. But when I say, "I love you!" and they reply, "I know that! I love you too, Mommy!" I realize that I've done some things right.

Wow! Just putting these things into words and writing them down has boosted my confidence in myself. Forget about my handicaps, I've got a lot to offer and I've barely gotten started! I feel empowered, so watch out storm because you don't stand a chance of keeping me down or holding me back!

Now it's your turn to give it a try. And don't be surprised or feel bad if, for just a little while, you allow yourself to forget about those dark clouds overhead and realize that you are smiling at yourself when you look in the mirror. Grab that Paddle of Confidence because you do have what it takes to use it. I'll see you in the sun!

24

The Most Beautiful Paddle

"Being deeply loved by someone gives you strength, loving someone deeply gives you courage."
- Lao Tzu

Love, the most beautiful paddle in your boat. Don't just pick it up, embrace it, because when all else fails, love can still prevail. Love can be reason enough to hang on through the darkest of nights. It can move us to do things that we wouldn't dare try otherwise, to fight when all common sense says to give up, and to believe in the unbelievable. It can allow us to see beauty even in the midst of the darkness. Love is such a powerful and valuable commodity that, if necessary, we will spend our whole lives searching for it because we instinctively know that it alone can make all of the difference and can make our journeys worthwhile.

In fact, our longing for love and our hopes to be rescued by it can consume us. It is so easy to get caught up in waiting and looking for love that we may find ourselves constantly scanning the horizon, hoping to see it coming to save us. But there is a great danger in doing so; by always looking for love "out there," we just might miss it in our boats, sitting quietly beside us. You see, love doesn't save us from the storms, love goes through them with us.

The appearance of the Paddle of Love can be deceiving. One would expect something with such value and power to stand out. But love often looks so ordinary that we can easily overlook, misjudge, or simply not appreciate it. Once we learn to recognize and value love in all of its forms, this beautiful tool can make our storms less threatening and our journeys brighter and more peaceful. It is the same as when a little child wants to climb into bed with Mommy and Daddy during a storm, even though they can't make the thunder and lightning go away or truly protect him from the danger. Somehow the feeling of comfort that comes from just having that love and support next to him makes the night bearable, and his fear loses out to rest.

The love that is ours to lean on can present itself in many forms and embodiments. It has a diversity of faces, though few of them look heroic. It can be ever-present, offering security with its reliability, or it can sneak up on you and catch you off guard with its sensitivity and thoughtfulness.

I never did see love coming in towards me from some distant horizon. I would simply turn around and there it was, in its many different voices and wearing many different faces. Yes, love can be strong and bold, but most of the distance and the power that I got from this paddle came from it appearing in its most subtle, sweet, unselfish, and everyday forms.

I've opened my eyes to see love standing over my hospital bed. I've felt it in the hands that held mine while I was waiting for test results. It has encouraged me through warm hugs from friends and family. I've heard about it in the accounts of the prayer dance that an Indian tribe held for me and the prayer requests traveling across the country from trucker to trucker, both for me to survive the encephalitis. I saw it again and again as I read the sweet words and the inspiring messages in the dozens of cards that were sent to me. It is kind of hard to give up when that many people are encouraging and rooting for you. Love was visible in the faces of the more than fifty people who showed up at my church one Sunday night for a prayer service that was held to ask God to heal my eyes. I didn't receive a healing that night; instead I received a lesson in how beautiful this paddle can be.

I've heard love more times than I could ever count in the voice of my husband as he automatically reads subtitles on television and movie screens to me because he knows that I can't see them. I've discovered it on physically trying days when he can tell that I'm struggling and asks with compassion, "There's nothing I can do, is there?" And then he'll hug me to let me know he's there, even if it's to do nothing but love me.

Love used to appear as a tiny, little girl with a ponytail asking her mommy if she needed help. It now shows up as a teenager in makeup who, although having never been asked to do so, will often walk in front of me so that she can send warnings back over her shoulder if the pavement is uneven or if there is something that I could trip on. I've heard it in that same teenager's voice saying, "Oh, no, you don't!" when I pick up something that might be hard for me to carry, as she rushes to take it from me. And I've seen it in the "I love you" text messages that have come from her phone on emotionally hard days.

I've witnessed love when Faith stops mid-stride to ask, "Is there anything that I can help you with, Mommy?" or says, "Oh, I'll get that," as we are unloading from the van. I've heard it as she has called after me hundreds of times, "Please be careful, Mommy." And I've seen it in the love that pours from her eyes as she tells me, "Good night."

It has come in the sound of my daughters' voices as directions are read to me off the back of a cake box because the print is too small for me to read on my own. Again and again, I've heard love as one of them asks, "Do you want me to fill that form out for you?" or says, "Mommy, you need to sign right here on this line." No, I won't be scanning the horizon for love to come to me from some distant place. I've discovered it's already here with me every day.

I got to feel love each time Mom drove across town to take grandchildren to their activities or me out to eat and shopping when I couldn't drive. When babies were carried upstairs and diapers were changed so that I could have a break from the pain and difficulty, I recognized it. Love came in the form of my brother, Scott, not only when he brought the Egg McMuffin to me in the hospital, but also when he met us at the emergency room one night when I had a panic attack and was sure that I was having a relapse. The doctors said that everything was fine, but for some reason, I wanted to hear it from Scott, not from the doctors, my husband, my mother, or my father. I wanted him to tell me if I was going to die or not. Somehow the complete trust I had that he would tell me the truth, even if the truth wasn't pretty, represented the love between us more than words ever could.

I thought I was looking at my father as he was worrying that a diaper bag and a pizza box were too much for me to handle, then I realized that it was the Paddle of Love I was seeing. The same man who had encouraged me to "go for it" by diving onto the ground, had his instinct to protect and take care of his little girl kick in, and love surprised me. And I'm certain that I heard it as Dad's voice when I called to ask if I could come tell my story at the church he pastored. He simply said, "Be here next Sunday for the 11:00 service," with no questions asked.

Love flew home with my brother, Matt, to be at the hospital with me, and it had to have been present whenever he would help hold me up to go to the bathroom. I saw it again when I read an interview about his career in the newspaper. In it, he described the day I woke up from the coma as the happiest day of his life.

You can see love by pulling out any one of my family's In Case of Emergency call lists and looking at where my stepdad's cell phone number is listed. Knowing that we can depend on Bill, not only to answer the call, but to be willing to drop anything to respond to whatever the need is, has given us all security during life's storms.

I've seen firsthand the magic of the Paddle of Love, the strength that you can receive from it, and just how far it can take you. And there is nothing that I would trade for that understanding.

So whatever storm you are going through at this time, ask yourself if love is what has gotten you this far. Or have you been so focused on "out there" or so busy fretting over the dark clouds overhead that you have disregarded the force that waits next to you? Is it time to take another look around, one that might allow you to recognize and draw strength from this paddle? Maybe you have been expecting the trumpets to sound and the stallion to come charging in carrying your hero or heroine, while the title track plays in the background. That would be wonderful if it happened, but we sure would miss out on many of life's small joys if just one big moment was all that we got. Ever notice that we never see what happens after the ride off into the sunset? Happily Ever After might turn out to be quite boring.

I'm not discouraging you from believing in your dreams, just don't miss out on the love that you may come across while waiting, love that appears as the hand that quietly holds yours when you are scared or as the voice of a friend encouraging you. Don't fail to notice it in the smile of a child or hear it in a compliment from a family member on an especially hard day. Feel love in the hug or the high-five given to you as you celebrate good news with someone. I think that stories with fairytale endings and beautiful theme songs are great, but keep in mind that in real life we usually find love working the hardest and most effectively in the quiet and uncelebrated twinklings of our days. It is in those moments that you will find your reasons and your strength to stay the course.

Understand that while this paddle might be extra special, it isn't meant to nor will it be able to replace the other paddles. Instead, the Paddle of Love is what can overcome our weaknesses and gives us the desire and the heart to use the others most effectively. Love helps us discover the boldness to look at the truth, the courage to face our fears, the confidence to believe in ourselves, and reasons to hope. Love doesn't replace the effort that it takes to paddle to where we want to be, it just makes doing so worthwhile.

Perhaps you are sitting there reading this with a heavy heart because you really don't have anyone to demonstrate love to you while you are going through the rough waters. Your eyes and your heart are both wide open to recognizing and appreciating any and all forms of love, but it just isn't there. Or maybe the fact that you don't have anyone to share the good and bad times of life with is the adversity that you are going through. Your loneliness is your storm. Well, put aside the sadness and keep reading because, boy, do I have great news for you!

My struggles have taught me an invaluable lesson. It is something that has gotten me through trials that nothing else could have, not even the love I felt from my husband, my children, my parents, or my family. It is a realization that has changed my life forever! It is this: the Paddle of Love has a reverse setting. It works just as well, if not better, when you are giving love rather than receiving it. To put it in the simplest way that I possibly can, I haven't fought through my adversities because my children loved me, I fought because I loved them.

This awareness came to me not that long ago when I was going through an emotionally down period. Terry and I had a lot of stress in our lives at the time and there was plenty to be down about. But I kept wondering why I wasn't coping with this set of circumstances as well as I had others that had been more serious than these. I pulled out my Awareness Paddle and tried to figure out what was going on.

Comparing notes of then and now, it hit me. During the other times, I was very busy passing along love to others. I didn't have time to be down. Yes, I was in pain and things were hard emotionally and physically, but I had something more important to occupy my mind, something more fun to think about. I had kids to love! First and foremost, there were my two beautiful girls and our crazy life. But there were also the neighborhood kids that would come over to play or do homework. The teens at my dad's church had filled up Tuesdays. At my church, hugs, lessons, and activities were a vital part of the rest of my week. It was hard to be miserable when some precious voice was often hollering, "Miss Christi!" Trouble has a way of getting overshadowed by smiles and laughter.

That was then, this is now. We have been dealing with financial hardships from closing down our business and are looking for other career opportunities, some health issues of mine have resurfaced and I have been in more pain and am having more physical challenges than I have in years. It has been stressful, but the stress in and of itself isn't the reason that I couldn't get out of my funk. The circumstances of my life had changed and I started letting myself float instead of paddling with my whole heart. My kids are older and have other things to do that don't involve me as much as they once did, we moved across town and we don't have neighborhood kids coming over as much, we haven't gotten involved in a new church, and my teen program ended years ago as most of the group went off to college. To sum it up, my Paddle of Love wasn't being used on its highest reverse setting anymore and therefore, I had less to fight for, more time to think about myself, and fewer smiles to counter the turbulence. That meant that none of my other paddles were able to work as effectively either. No wonder I was worn out, I had been paddling in circles.

I want to emphasize that using the reverse setting on this paddle does not apply to abusive or unhealthy relationships! Many people that are in these types of relationships think that if they just love their abuser or the other person enough, it will all work out. No! Love should help you make it through the storm, not be the cause of it. If you are in a relationship that is itself a threat to any part of your well-being, put the Paddle of Love down for now. Pick up the Paddle of Awareness and take a long hard look at the truth. When you're ready, pick up the Paddle of Love once more and use it to love yourself first. Then you can truly enjoy the rest of your journey.

However, if your circumstances are "normal," but you are just at a point in your life where you don't have anyone loving or demonstrating love to you, you should know that this paddle can still work its magic. How? You be the one to show love to someone or for something. This might require that you get off your butt, quit your pity-party, pull up the anchor, and pick up the paddles that we have previously discussed. But if you are willing to do that, you will find more joy than you thought possible.

Whenever you feel overwhelmed, whether it will last for a short or an extended period, pull the Paddle of Love out of the water, put it on the highest reverse setting, and then try rowing with it every chance you get. Demonstrate and feel love all throughout the day. You can't run out of it, so start giving it away and see where doing so takes you.

"I'm not like that," you say.

My response? "Give me a break! It doesn't get any easier than this."

Find an elderly neighbor to befriend. Don't know of any? Walk into a nursing home and tell a worker that you want to visit someone who seldom gets visitors. Then go introduce yourself to that person and ask if he or she would mind if you sat down for a minute. Ask questions about his or her past. Or if you want something even easier, most nursing homes will have residents sitting in the hallways. Just walk around saying hello and squeezing hands. The precious looks that you will get will make you sorry when it's time for you to leave.

Offer to mentor a child or become a tutor. Volunteer at a shelter or food pantry. If you don't know how to find out about any of these ideas, take it from a preacher's kid, here's what you do: pick up the phone and call a pastor at a local church. Tell him or her that you want to volunteer in the community, but don't know how to get started. If you happen, God forbid, to get a pastor that doesn't seem enthusiastic about helping you get plugged into something, thank him for his time, with love of course, and call another church. That particular minister might be facing his own storm and has misplaced his Paddle of Love.

If you just aren't there yet, start with something else. Get a new pet, send out birthday cards, or make it your mission to say, "Have a nice day!" or "God bless you!" to as many people as you can each day. If you really want to feel better, show love through random acts of kindness to complete strangers. One of my favorite things to do is to find something to compliment about the person standing next to me in line. "I love the color of that shirt!" is an easy one. And speaking of lines, how about letting the mom, with the kids who are squirming and wiggling with impatience, go in front of you at the grocery store checkout? No, not just when she only has a few items, but when her cart is packed full. You will be paid back a hundred times over by the looks of surprise, shock, and heartfelt gratitude shining in the eyes of the recipients of your love.

In between those times, keep using the Paddle of Love. "Did you forget that I'm the one who doesn't have anyone," you remind me with a sigh. "so who is it I'm supposed to keep loving?"

My answer is, "It doesn't have to be a 'who.' Love anything and everything." You can love the clouds, the flowers, the changing of the leaves, pizza, the beach, art, and video games. Faith loves gymnastics and singing. Ansley loves dancing and trying new foods. Terry loves playing the guitar and writing songs. I love listening to my favorite songs, especially sappy love songs and Terry's, the North Georgia Mountains and a certain lake there, Coca-Cola, beautiful sunsets, horses, chocolate chip cookie dough, the color purple, seafood, newborn babies, America, French vanilla cappuccinos from QuikTrip convenience stores, and swimming pools.

Maybe it's reading, playing or watching sports,

a certain kind of music, fixing things, cooking, gardening, crafts, or going to the movies that moves you. You can love your bed, your TV, or walking around the neighborhood in the quietness of the morning. The point is to feel the happiness that only love can bring and to spend some positive emotional energy that will propel you forward. And when you love, love, and then love some more, you will find that the distance you've covered from where you were to where you are now is amazing!

Because, you see, what makes the Paddle of Love so beautiful isn't that you don't have the storms and the adversities anymore, it's that when you do get around to noticing them, they just don't seem as harsh and threatening as they once did. You will have discovered the magical power that this paddle holds. Love can cut through even the thickest and darkest of storm clouds to let the sun shine through and it can calm the waters beneath you, letting you find peace in the journey ahead. But be prepared. When you put this paddle into use, you just may find that people start asking how you manage to stay so upbeat when you are going through so much. Do me a favor, pass on the joy, the magic, and the power. Tell them about the most beautiful paddle.

25

The Paddle of Celebration

*"Celebrating is an acceptable way
for adults to imitate children."
- Christi Kasha*

Ready to have some fun? Then pull out the Paddle of Celebration and stick it in the water. No, no, no, don't stop to think about this one or try to analyze it. Just grab it, plunge it in, start rowing, and see where it takes you!

"You want me to celebrate in the middle of this nightmare?" you ask dubiously.

"I sure do. The hard times might be just that- hard. But dwelling on the negative instead of looking at the positive doesn't move you away from the negative, it only draws you to it."

Life is truly a matter of perspective and what you take away from this period in your life is totally up to you. Will you look back on it and think of how your storm robbed you of your happiness and took so much from you or will you see it as a time when you learned a great deal, especially about yourself, when you discovered the things that matter the most to you, when you laughed often, and when you got to celebrate joy?

I can't think of a better time to rejoice than in the middle of tough times. It's kind of like laughing in adversity's face, not to mention that getting excited and celebrating something brings about more things to be happy about. When you change your focus to what's positive, suddenly you'll begin noticing more and more positive things. The kind of happiness that results can quickly turn difficulty into an exciting challenge.

"Great, but how do you expect me to use this paddle if there's nothing to celebrate? And look at me. What do I have to be to be excited about?"

Just as it was with what you should love, my answer is once again, "Anything and everything!" If you want to find yourself feeling the warmth of the sun as quickly as possible, quit sitting around waiting for The Big Ones. Start getting excited and find something to celebrate right now. Yes, you should keep making a big deal over those meaningful milestones, but remember that the silly, trivial stuff is what most of life is made up of, and therefore, it deserves to be celebrated as well.

Most of us do what I'm talking about as second nature. Anytime something brings a smile to your face or causes you to feel all warm inside, you are in a momentary state of celebration. But in the busyness of life and in stressful times, we tend to give little thought to those moments. We have, after all, more important matters that demand our attention. By simply learning to tune into those emotions and allowing ourselves time to really feel and enjoy them, we will find ourselves celebrating life.

Maybe because I was in "recovery" from the encephalitis, it seemed more appropriate and somewhat expected to get excited over any and every improvement that I had. With tears of joy running down my face, I looked in the mirror one day to admire the earrings that I had just put in. It wasn't the earrings that I was emotional about, it was my accomplishment of having put them in by myself for the first time in many months. That deserved celebrating! It still takes me what seems like forever to put a pair in, especially when I can remember throwing them in while stopped at a red light. Still, every time the back is put on the second one, a tiny smile passes across my face as I celebrate how far I've come. There has never been anyone more excited over finding out certain magazines and books come in large print. And there aren't words to describe my joy over getting a big screen TV. Terry still claims that he wanted to get it just to help me out. Yeah, right. Balancing on the bed to clean the glass on the picture hanging above it, being able to read a menu, realizing that I could stand on one foot for a few seconds, and cutting my meat by myself were all more reasons to celebrate. Yes, my answer is, "anything and everything!"

I have always loved swimming, but since being sick, the water pressure has bothered me. It was too much on my nerves, I suppose. So I would say, "1, 2, 3, go!" and make myself get into the pool where I would get acclimated to the pressure, but it wasn't the same kind of fun as it had always been. For me, swimming was supposed to be relaxing, refreshing, and exuberant, not sad. So this year at the season's first swim, I realized as I walked in timidly that the water felt great, like it used to! People probably wondered what was going on as I was laughing and crying at the same time. I had regained something that I had missed more than anyone knew, and they were watching a celebration take place.

One of the sweetest memories I have of celebrating is from Matt's wedding eight years ago. Terry and I were dancing to one of "our songs." I looked up at him and saw tears. "What's wrong?" I asked, worried.

He smiled so tenderly at me and said quietly, "You're dancing. You're just plain dancing. I'm not having to support you. You're just dancing."

If there was something to celebrate, we did, and it turned ordinary tasks into magical moments. It's the power that the feelings of "I can!" "I did!" and "I will!" bring to our lives.

So give it a try! "Na-na-na-boo-boo" your adversity. Celebrate every chance you get. Celebrate the big things and the ordinary things. Celebrate things happening that you have been hoping for and things that you have been dreading that don't come to pass. You can celebrate quietly, act like a nut, or come across as an emotional wreck.

If you are struggling financially, celebrate finding enough change for a cup of coffee. Or when you go to the mailbox and find a coupon for something you use and no bills, do a little dance on the way back to the house. If you're looking for a job, get excited about a new job listing or a lead that someone has told you about. If you're sick, celebrate how good a shower makes you feel. If you are not up to your to-do list, celebrate the comfortable sofa. Get worked up over a good hair day. If you have physical limitations, celebrate feeling up to sweeping the floor or folding a load of laundry. If you are lonely, celebrate meeting someone new that you got to talk to and that might become a friend. And there's always beautiful sunsets, a call from a friend, the clothes you want to wear being clean and fitting well, a special song on the radio, a funny email when you are down, your favorite TV show coming on, and ice cream to get excited about.

So, go ahead, grab the Paddle of Celebration, start rowing, and notice how many things you will find along the way that are worth rejoicing over. Be sure to bring your smile because you will be surprised at how fun your journey will become and how much joy you can discover in the middle of a storm. You might end up celebrating not only making it through the night and reaching your destination, but also the journey itself. And if you happen to see a woman along the way who is either crying over something goofy or dancing around like a nut, come on over, say hello, and we'll celebrate together.

26

The Paddle of Laughter

*"Laughter gives us distance.
It allows us to step back from an event,
deal with it and then move on."*
- Bob Newhart

While the Paddle of Laughter might not change the situation or eliminate the problem, it does have the ability to change your demeanor. Laughter is both healing and fun, and it can be a great tool to use in overcoming adversity and in celebrating. So use it often and unsparingly.

I discovered that one of the best remedies for making me feel better when I'm coping with difficulty is to pull this paddle out and use it with my family and my friends - by laughing at myself! I offer great material for many jokes and the damage to my nervous system has been a super source of family entertainment. My girls have gotten a kick out of poking me somewhere on my body and then having me surprise them with where it was that I felt the resulting sensation the most. For instance, they might softly pinch my left forearm and I would feel a resulting tingle in my right thigh. My lack of balance, coordination, and mobility have prompted them to beg for me to please not dance in front of their friends. Even I have to admit that their imitations of me doing certain physical activities, like jogging or reading, have been not only accurate, but quite humorous as well. Comments referring to "the blind woman" are a regular occurrence in our house. Some examples of the abuse I have to endure are, "It's pretty sad when you have to ask a blind woman for directions," "You know that you aren't very hung up on your appearance when you let your blind, half paralyzed wife cut your hair," and "Mommy, maybe you're not the best person to get to proofread this." Oh, yes, there has been much laughter.

Allowing yourself to find humor in and to make fun of your adversity is a great way to vent. You get to complain all you want, share your troubles, deal with the harsh reality of your situation, and somehow come away smiling and feeling more positive. There needs to be a time for talking seriously about the things that are painful and stressful to us and to those going through the storms with us, but sometimes just being able to laugh at the situation and to be lighthearted about something awful is a great coping mechanism. If you are dealing with an illness or a disease, laugh with your spouse about something goofy that a member of the medical staff innocently said. If you are confused about which direction to take your life in, create a grab bag with options that are totally off-the-wall. If your finances have been pushed to the limit, while eating dinner with your family, try making up your own version of "The Twelve Days of Christmas," substituting gifts that you could afford. My version might go: "On the twelfth day of Christmas my true love gave to me twelve broken eggshells, eleven spaghetti noodles, ten miniature marshmallows, nine paper towels..." Uh, oh, now I'm on a roll, so I'll just stop there.

Humor reminds us that we can still feel joy, despite the pain and it offers proof that fun times are not only ahead of us, but are available to us where we are. When we are having fun, the tasks at hand don't seem as daunting and our troubles seem less discouraging. There is a reason the dwarfs whistled while they worked.

Like love, laughter should never hurt. Laughing at someone is a completely different ballgame than laughing with someone. That kind of demeaning fun is not healing anyone's pain, it is just being used to mask your own. Making fun of the situation or the people involved is only okay if it doesn't make them feel bad about themselves. If you aren't sure, ask. You'll most likely be able to tell the truth by the response you receive. It's obvious that it's okay with me because I often start it. But if you are the subject of the teasing and you don't like it or it makes you feel uncomfortable, let people know. They'll almost always apologize and stop.

My advice on using the Paddle of Laughter is not to look for an instruction manual because one doesn't exist. Just pull it out when the time is right and there is a need for it. How it works best can vary widely with different storms and even with your mood for the day. This paddle's purpose is to distract you from the storm clouds and to make them seem less threatening. If laughing about your struggles makes you feel worse, then put the paddle down for now.

Wait! Before you do, let's consider something else. Maybe it's not laughter itself that's painful, maybe it's your viewpoint. You might not be at a place where you can see any humor in what you are going through, it's too serious, too painful, too scary, and that's okay. But that doesn't mean that laughing wouldn't feel good. There are other sources that can provide you with humor that will help you heal. Watch funny movies or TV shows, buy a new joke book, or sign up for a Joke of the Day or a humor column email. Try getting together in person or over the phone with longtime friends and family members, siblings and cousins work best for this, and tell old stories on each other. You can even take a few minutes to stop by the greeting card aisle at the store to just read some of the funny cards. If there's one you love, buy it for yourself. If it worked today, it will work again tomorrow, so bring the laughter home with you. The one that I gave myself for my birthday several years ago is hanging on my bulletin board. It was intended to make fun of the recipient's age, but I saw another, more applicable personal meaning in the message. Inside was a button to wear that read, "I've survived damn near everything!"

I readily admit that I'm kind of a nutcase. My family would argue over the "kind of" part. I can make myself laugh over nothing. I'll make up silly jingles in my head, come up with a new word that just sounds funny to say, or my favorite, I love to slide down the staircase in our house on my tush. I learned the hard way to make sure that I'm wearing long pants when I do because carpet burns on your legs can ruin the magic of the moment. Now, you don't have to go stair-sliding with me or make up nonsensical rhyming songs, but find something to bring a smile to your face, even if it's just for a few moments. Here's another idea for you to try- buy a can of whipped cream and squirt it directly into your mouth. It is extremely hard to keep from smiling while you are doing that. Trust me!

The Paddle of Laughter might not make your storm go away, but it will certainly cause your adversity to shake its head in confusion, and it just might turn a tough journey into an enjoyable adventure. So pull it out and use it every chance you get. It's certainly worth giving it a shot. Hey, is that you whistling while you paddle?

27

The Paddle of Compassion

"I used to do the right thing if the opportunity presented itself. Now, I look for opportunities to do the right thing."
- Terry Kasha

One of the most positive, far-reaching outcomes from going through adversity is the chance to learn how to use your Paddle of Compassion in a way that people who haven't struggled aren't able to do. There are those who are too bitter over their own struggles to want to pick this paddle up, but, oh, what they are missing out on! It won't dismiss our own storm's fury or alleviate our battles, but somehow holding it can empower us and has a magical, miraculous way of turning our journeys into something valuable. We all want to make a difference in this world, to feel as though we matter and that we have something to contribute. But most of us see ourselves as not having anything worthwhile to offer or that we're not in a position to give while we are coping with our own troubles. However, we need to understand that is exactly when this paddle works the best. Your adversity is your advantage. It can be your guide in how to make the world a little better and a little brighter for all of us.

"Been there, done that, got the t-shirt" can be very beneficial in reaching out to others. People can care, but there is something special when another person understands. It's the reason that my friend, Kim, and I bonded and can share easily our vision difficulties. It's why support groups exist and the reason that my sister-in-law, Denise, volunteered at the hospital after losing her babies. Who better to help parents who have lost a little one than another parent who understands in a way that no one else can? One of the things that makes this paddle so special is that the more you use it to help others, the more you help yourself, as doing so proves that the struggles you've been through don't have to be in vain and that your journey can have meaning and purpose to it.

My tough times have taught me to look at the people who cross my path during the course of any given day with more understanding and empathy than I would have before. Do I always demonstrate it as I should? I'll be the first to say no, so there's no need to ask my children, my husband, or other family members. Show some compassion towards me, okay? But have you ever stopped to notice how few of the people around you are smiling? I find myself thinking about what they might be going through or how they might be feeling. The reason for this is, and my stomach tightens as I admit it, that I know all too well what it is like to feel insecure, awkward, incompetent, scrutinized, doubted, talked about, and an outsider. It breaks my heart to think that someone else might be feeling those things.

My experiences and challenges have taught me not to assume too quickly that things are as they appear at first glance. For example, I'll say to myself or to Terry as we come upon a person who is driving slowly or in a somewhat out-of-the-ordinary manner, "Be patient. He might be wearing new bi-optics and not be used to them yet." or "Maybe she's having trouble reading the street signs." Why? It's simple: been there, done that, got the t-shirt. Then I send the driver a heart-to-heart message telling them, "Take your time. I'm not in a hurry. We're good."

Or I might see a store clerk looking grumpy, and I'll find myself automatically wondering if she has been standing too long or if he recently got bad news. It's no excuse to be rude to customers, but who knows how we would behave if we were in her or his shoes. "You look like you're having one of those days," I'll often say. Sometimes I'll get the story, but often I'll just get a grunt, a nod, or a "Yeah," because too many people don't know how to act when someone shows compassion towards them. "Well, I hope it gets better. Have a good day," I'll offer as I leave.

Another driver who is speeding or cutting in front of me is no longer irritating. It might be that he or she might be racing to the hospital to meet a spouse before the test or the surgery begins. I feel good slowing down to let them over. And, yes, it's quite possible that the driver is just a teenager making dumb decisions about driving while spreading his wings. I'm not in much of a position to judge him either, for that was me once. "Thank you, God, for the protective angels I must have had. Please send that person some," I'll pray as the car makes it safely into the lane ahead of me.

I'm going to let some of you in on a secret. My apologies to those of you who already know all too well what I'm talking about for exposing our little cover up. But I'm hoping that by doing so, it will help all of us recognize that things aren't always what they seem. Here it is: We, who have been through or who are going through trials and tribulations, aren't always completely upfront about what we are feeling or thinking. It can be embarrassing, too emotional, or just hard to explain. We may think that people won't understand, and sometimes, we just haven't figured out what's going on ourselves. So to those who aren't already aware of this, please keep in mind that there might be more behind someone's statements and both their actions and reactions than how it first appears.

If someone doesn't accept an invitation eagerly, perhaps it isn't that she doesn't really want to go. Maybe there are other issues that she is embarrassed to talk about. My grandmother resisted going to Faith's gymnastics competition not long ago. "Hmm...," I thought, "Her reasons aren't adding up. There's more to it." After some questions, the truth came out. She was afraid that the gym might have bleacher style seating that would be hard for her to manage with her bad knee. I assured her that the seating would not be an issue and she ended up having a great time. The reason I was tuned into this is because whenever I have plans to go somewhere, I find myself pausing to think over and evaluate the situation. I'll consider the facilities and if I can manage them okay on my own. With many events, I stop to think about how much walking and activity will be involved. Going to a new place by myself, I wonder if I'll have trouble finding it or if I'll be able to read the restaurant's menu if the lighting is bad. Now, I'm adventurous enough that I'll go no matter what answers I come up with and, of course, I'm always more at ease if Terry or another family member is going to be with me. But having to do this can put a damper on the excitement that I might otherwise feel.

If you are inviting someone who has been through a storm to do something, be patient and understand that their considerations might be things that you would never even think about. If your friend just lost someone through death or a breakup, going to certain places or areas might be painful for them. A simple lunch could be a major financial burden to a friend that just lost his job. A certain type of movie might be pushing the limits for the person suffering from post-traumatic stress disorder. For someone like me, an outing to the park or a walk around the neighborhood is a big deal. So if you receive an unexpected negative or hesitant response to an invitation that you have given, ask some questions and offer an alternative activity.

If you are the invitee, remember that most of us have been through some kind of storm and would understand or, at the very least, respect that there are reasons for your concerns. Try doing one of two things, depending on your comfort level and your own understanding of that knot in your stomach. Either explain to the person who invited you what you are worried about or simply tell him or her that you aren't sure what's going on yourself and you'd rather not try to talk about the specifics, but there are reasons you're hesitant to say yes. Then offer another place or activity that you would be more comfortable doing.

Several years back, we found out that a good friend of Ansley's was going to decline her birthday party invitation. I "discovered" the family was struggling financially and she didn't want to, or her parents thought that she shouldn't, come without a present. Realizing what was going on and feeling compassion because of the tough financial times I've been through, both as a child and as an adult, I discussed with my daughter what we should do. With her eager permission, a quick email was sent out to everyone saying that in lieu of presents, we'd love for something to be donated to a local charity. Problem solved. Presents still arrived with some guests, but no one felt awkward walking in without one. And it was one of Ansley's most memorable parties!

Yes, what we've gone through can help us to recognize the same in another person and to connect with them in a deeper way. Several years back, Ansley was competing in an ice skating competition. I had gone out to the car for something, braving the weekend's awful weather; well, I use the word awful from the perspective of a southern girl, okay? Anyway, I was coming back inside, dodging the sleet and trying to avoid the slushy ice in front of the arena. As I started up the concrete stairs leading to the front door, I was about to pass a woman with her head bowed against the cold. She glanced my way. There was something about her hesitation and the look in her eyes that I picked up on and painfully recognized. "Ma'am, do you need any help with these stairs? They look a little slippery."

"Oh, God bless you!" she said with a deep sigh of relief. "There's no handrail and I have trouble walking. I didn't know how I was going to get up them."

"Well, to be honest, I have had some physical troubles that made walking hard for me too. I recognized that look on your face."

She grabbed hold of my arm and together we cautiously and slowly conquered the slick, icy, wet steps. Once we were safely inside, she hugged me tightly and thanked me repeatedly. "I don't know what I would have done. People were running by so fast trying to get out of the weather that they didn't stop. I was scared that I would slip and break something."

"There's no need to thank me," I told her. "I'm just glad that I was there. I've had to hold on to someone so many times, it's nice to be able to have a chance to pay it forward. I guess not being able to move as quickly as I used to can be a good thing."

My new friend and I exchanged addresses and said good-bye with another hug. I never did admit that I was praying as hard as I could for stability and strength while we were going up those stairs. I think she would understand and would forgive me. The funny thing was that I felt stronger and more balanced than I normally did. Focusing on the needs of another made me forget about my own inadequacies. My storms had allowed me to make a difference in the life of a complete stranger, even if it was for just a moment, and for that I am grateful. I may have lost a lot while I was gaining handicaps, but maybe God will use them to give me clearer vision and better balance when it comes to recognizing certain needs of others. "Use me as you need me, God," is my request.

Sometimes the most meaningful ways that God can use us and that we can show compassion are the simplest. I helped a lady up a few stairs, she said she would never forget me. My mother still speaks of the friends and family who came to the hospital from all over when I was sick, many bringing trays of food for my family. I know of my brothers and their wives sleeping in chairs in the hospital waiting room so that Terry wouldn't be at the hospital by himself during the night. Terry has also told me how much it meant to him when his brother, Steve, sat with me in my hospital room all night long so that Terry could go home and try to get a good night's sleep. No, compassion isn't measured by the grandness of the gesture, but by the goodness of the heart.

I am reminded of a song that touches me every time I hear it. The song, by the incredible country music group, Alabama, is titled "Angels Among Us." Its inspiring lyrics relate how when there has been trouble and hard times in the singer's life, there has always been somebody that offered comfort. The "angel" might have been a stranger that said something nice or a friend calling, but no matter who it was, they offered hope. The song goes on to say that there are angels among us that are sent to us to teach us things and to offer us light when our lives seem dark.

Thank you to all of the angels that have touched my heart and impacted my life. And, God, please let my storms act as training grounds for learning how to use my Paddle of Compassion, so that I can be an angel to someone else during their dark hours.

Whatever storm you are facing or trying to understand, the Paddle of Compassion can take you to that place inside of yourself where you'll discover all that you have to give. As you row along, you will come to see how what you have experienced can help you to reach out and understand others in a way that many people can't. So throw compassion out into the rough waters that you are paddling through. By doing so you will start a ripple effect that just may bounce off of another angel and come back to you at the exact time you need it. Compassion, whether we are receiving or giving it, pushes us forward towards the place where the sun is shining.

I wish adversity wasn't something that we have to deal with, but it is a part of life. So we might as well use our storms and our willingness to understand others' journeys in a way that makes the skies a little brighter and the world a little better for all of us. I want to encourage you to give it a try. And trusting that you will, let me just go ahead and say, "Thank you for using your Paddle of Compassion to make a difference!"

28

The Paddle of Gratitude

"Give thanks for a little and you will find a lot."
- The Hausa of Nigeria

Now, if you really want to paddle through this storm as quickly and as easily as possible, if you want to conquer your fears and find many reasons to celebrate and to laugh, then get intimately familiar with the Paddle of Gratitude. When you can recognize all that you have to be thankful for, even in the midst of your world falling apart, then you will know that your difficulties have lost their hold on you. If you can declare, "Thank you for today!" when the storm clouds are overhead and the rain is blowing in your face, with just as much sincerity as when the sun is shining and soft breezes are caressing your skin, then there is very little that will pose a threat to your well-being. Will there be sadness, pain, fear, and heartbreak in the miles and the years ahead of you? Of course, for such things are a natural part of life's makeup. But when you come to understand that negative issues can have positive impacts, you'll know that you have gained the upper hand and, come what may, the morning sun will rise to find you thriving and filled with true happiness.

My handicaps and limitations have brought more daily struggles into my life than I would have ever thought possible. Some of them are tough to deal with emotionally, some are physically painful, and some are just a pain in the butt. However, the experiences and lessons that they have left me with, I will forever be grateful for. It's possible that I would have had the same type of outlook on life had I not gone through these storms. I've always been one to see the glass as half full instead of half empty. I give credit to my parents for that, both through my upbringing and my DNA. But if I hadn't been forced to fight to get to where I am, I wonder if I would value and appreciate parts of my life as much and in the same way that I do today. Would I have the same fondness for running kids around, easy-to-read signs, helpful employees, running errands, places to sit down in stores, handrails on stairs, and a large television screen? Would before and after school hugs, helping with homework, attending competitions, pillow fights, and bedtime prayers be so precious? Yes, my life could be easier, but at what cost?

I have my adversity to thank for all of the times that I have needed help keeping my balance, and therefore, getting to hold Terry's hand and feel his arms around me more than I would have otherwise. I've learned that fighting life's storms together can strengthen bonds that were already strong. Being as independent as I am, I might have never known how incredible it can be to know that you can count on someone to be there and to keep right on loving you even when you are at your worst. And my worst was pretty bad! But now I know. I found out that a hug can heal better than medicine and that the "I love you" sign in sign language, held up across a room or as a school bus pulls away, can sometimes say more than words.

The strong winds that have threatened to knock me over are the same ones that have blown priceless secrets in to me. They've told me how happiness is found not in things, but in our experiences, and how joy is hiding behind the small and ordinary parts of our lives, like a child's squeals of "Higher, higher!" on a swing, a handmade Mother's Day card, bubble baths, and picking out and decorating a Christmas tree together, then watching your child's face as you plug the lights in for the first time. Happiness can be discovered in tickle fights, practicing for a school solo a hundred times in the car, or making cake batter for the sole reason of eating it raw. Yes, I could have taken an easier route and there have been days when I wished that I had. But looking back, no thanks! I ended up taking the most beautiful one.

My troubles did get me some special attention and being treated like royalty, even if for just a short time, wasn't all that bad and is worth a thank you or two. I'm warning you, to this day, you had better not even think of taking the last seat and leave me standing if my mother is around. And while we're on the subject of parents, I would like to apologize to the other people who were waiting in the emergency room the night I made the mistake of twisting my ankle in front of my father. It didn't matter if you had been waiting for hours or even if you were having a heart attack, which Dad himself has had. As far as he was concerned, this minor, and I do emphasize minor, injury might somehow be related to the virus from a year earlier and could be a sign of something else going on. Why the medical staff had not put out the code for a panicked father and then respond and rush me back immediately, he just could not understood. Sorry, everyone. I tried to calm him down, I promise.

One of my sweetest "royal" memories is one that I keep waiting for a repeat of. My whole family was celebrating my birthday at an all-you-can-eat seafood restaurant. Crab legs, my favorite food, were included, and I was in heaven. But it had been only a short time since my paralyzation, and the limited use of my left arm and hand were causing a challenge when it came to getting the meat out. It wasn't stopping my enjoyment and the extra effort was well worth the reward. But my wonderful brothers took pity on me and took over my plate. They began cracking and removing the scrumptious meat and piling it up on my plate so that all that was left for me to do was to dip it in the melted butter before devouring it. Let's just say that the restaurant did not make a profit off my meal that evening and that I did a good bit of moaning on the way home. I'm still not sure if my brothers were being nice to me for my birthday, were feeling sorry for me, or if they simply wanted to get home sometime before morning, and I don't really care. I doubt that Queen Elizabeth herself has ever felt more spoiled, but I can guarantee that she hasn't appreciated being pampered more than I did that evening. Hey, Matt and Scott, for my birthday this year, I had a thought...

Using the Paddle of Gratitude will not only help you enjoy the journey while you are fighting through your adversity, but it can also be used to measure just how far you've traveled since the storm's inception. One day, while visiting my grandmother, I was coming down from the bedrooms on the second floor. In the middle of the staircase, I stopped short, gasped a deep breath, and started crying. In a flash, it had hit me where I was and what it meant. I looked down at what was in my arms; it was Faith, whom I had just gotten up from her nap. I realized that I was carrying my baby down the steps, the same steps that not all that long ago, I had to use the chair lift to just get myself up and down. The happiness and gratitude that came from realizing how far I had come were overwhelming! "Thank you, thank you, thank you!" I whispered as I continued down the steps, did a U-turn at the bottom, and went up and down again just because I could. There has rarely been a time in the last nine years when that moment hasn't come to mind as I was going up or down those stairs.

Find a then-and-now moment that you can turn to when you are feeling down or hopeless, one that will remind you of how far you have come and the difference your efforts have made, one that will give you something to be grateful for. Your then-and-now moment might even seem disheartening or discouraging to an outsider, but to you it represents progress. You might look at the empty drawer in your bathroom, the one that no longer contains a significant other's stuff. Someone else might think, "How sad, he's alone." But to you, it can be a reminder of how hard you had to work to let go of something that wasn't good for you. Now there's a place that's ready, in your bathroom and in your heart, to be filled. Good for you! Look how far you've come!

This Paddle of Gratitude was with me one rainy day when the girls and I were at the grocery store. Wet from taking our time walking in through the rain and catching raindrops on our tongues in the parking lot, we made an adventure out of picking out snacks for the following week and deciding what kind of cereal we wanted to choose this time. Out of the blue, it struck me how close I had come to not having this moment. "Oh, thank you, God! I don't ever want to forget how precious and valuable this is or take it for granted. Please don't ever let me forget." I prayed.

Months later, I found out that at some point I must have laid this paddle down. Somehow it ended up on the pasta aisle at that same Kroger. The girls and I were back shopping there, but this time Terry was with us. It was one of those days. I was in a bad mood, Ansley and Faith were fussing, and we certainly weren't having a fun adventure. As Terry pushed the cart, I went to retrieve a needed item from another aisle, as much to get away from the chaos as to complete the shopping list. Two rows over and I could still hear those little voices going at it. I couldn't find what I was looking for and my legs were hurting so badly with half of the store still to cover. I was frustrated to say the least. Then out of nowhere I found it- the Paddle of Gratitude. I stopped in my tracks. "I almost forgot! Oh, God, I'm so sorry! I said that I wouldn't, but I almost took this for granted. I almost forgot that this is what I lived for!" I located the needed item and limping, took it and the paddle back to the cart. I was anxious to see life's treasures that were there waiting for me.

"Mommy!" a little voice hollered.

"I'm ready to go!" her sister informed me.

Daddy sighed and shook his head. "You doing okay? You look like you're really hurting," he questioned.

"Yeah, I'm hurting, but I'm good, real good." I smiled, appreciating him looking out for me and his seemingly endless supply of patience.

Then I turned my attention to Ansley and Faith. "Girls, we can't go. We haven't had enough fun yet. Come on!" I started pushing the cart down the aisle. I hope our impromptu version of "Roll, Roll, Roll Your Cart" wasn't too annoying to the other customers. The shopping list completed, we left with a full cart, smiling kids, a bewildered father, and one very thankful mother.

Yes, happiness and gratitude can be hiding in the strangest places. We just have to remember and be willing to look for them.

Gratitude might not be able to change your adversity or your circumstances, but it can change your moments, your days, and your life. So for just a minute, do something crazy. Take your focus away from the wind, the waves, and everything you are worried about and switch your thoughts to gratitude. If this storm has been going on for a while, think about some positive things that it has brought into your life or that it has taught you. Perhaps you are closer to someone than you would have been otherwise. Maybe you have discovered qualities about yourself and an inner strength that you didn't know you possessed. Have you moved to a new area that you really like? Has your understanding of the meaning and the value of true love changed? Have you found ways to make a difference? Do you appreciate your friends and family more than you used to? Or perhaps it's something as simple as you realize not to bother taking things so seriously since doing so doesn't help anyway. Or it could be that you appreciate a good night's sleep more than ever.

If this is a new storm or you just want to be prepared for what might blow your way, you may not have had the chance to discover the secrets that only adversity can teach you. But you can go ahead and start finding joy with this paddle immediately. Look around you right now and pick out one thing to be thankful for. For me, at this moment I can hear the sounds of Terry playing his guitar and singing downstairs. I love that sound and it's been a while! Thank you! One of our favorite shows is coming on television tonight and we'll sit and watch it together. Sharing that time of just sitting on the sofa has come to mean so much to us since finances have kept us from being able to go out more. Thank you!

What about you? Have you found something yet? Need some hints? Light is coming from somewhere for you to be able to see these words. Be thankful for its source. You are probably the type of person who wants things to be the best that they can be or you wouldn't be reading this type of book. Give yourself a pat on the back. Or you might be reading it because someone gave or suggested it to you, showing they care. Appreciate their interest in you. By the way, I just want to take a second to thank you for reading it. I'm grateful for you!

Now it's your turn. Find another reason for gratitude and then another. Keep your paddle close by as you go through your days and use it every chance you get. Be thankful for a favorite old song that comes on the radio when you're feeling sad or that brings back happy memories. When someone holds the door open for you, look him in the eye and sincerely tell them, "Thanks," this time from your heart, not just from your manners. Appreciate a short line, an extra delicious lunch, a smile from a stranger, a beautiful sunset, or your favorite team winning. Be grateful for the hug you get, the word of encouragement, and getting a friend request from an old friend on Facebook. Feel and then verbalize your thankfulness for your job, a chance to get a new customer, the gallon of milk in the refrigerator and the food in the pantry. And when joy jumps out and surprises you, even if just for a fleeting moment, be thankful!

If you are willing to try paddling with gratitude during periods of difficulty, you will be amazed at how much easier your life will seem and how quickly you will find yourself under blue skies. Yeah, there might be a storm cloud here and there, but this paddle has a way of helping us navigate around them as we notice their mysterious beauty instead of their threatening elements. Then when the skies are clear, living with gratitude will bring even that much more effortless joy to our journey, and we will find ourselves eager to shout, "Thank you for today!"

29

The Paddle of Perspective

"The journey must be just as important as the destination. Otherwise, cars would not have backseat windows."
- Christi Kasha

My two-year-old daughter was scared of the rain and hearing it outside of her window caused short naps and the need for middle of the night comforting and consoling. The forecast for the upcoming week had Terry and I shaking our heads at the thought of the loss of sleep we could expect. One afternoon it was raining and she and I were going to wait with an umbrella for her sister to get off of the school bus. Then I had an idea. I put the umbrella aside, found her raincoat in the back of the closet, put it on her, and said, "Let's go play in the rain!" It was pouring and the raincoat offered little protection as we got soaked from splashing in puddles and walking in the water streaming down the side of the road. The bus was running late, so we passed the time by laughing and playing. The scary rain was transformed into something that brought happiness and laughter. We had just picked up the Paddle of Perspective.

None of us invite the rain, the thunder, or other elements that scare us into our lives. Still, we encounter and are forced to deal with life's storms time and time again. No matter how old we are, we still need comforting and consoling from time to time. But when even that doesn't help or isn't available, the Paddle of Perspective can change the effect a storm has on us, not by dispersing the dark clouds, but by adjusting our view of what the rain represents to us.

In the middle of inclement weather, one person might be angry, scared, frustrated, and think that life sucks; and for him it does. However, another man with the same conditions might view the lightning as beautiful, mystical, and exciting. Think of a storm chaser. He finds himself in awe, smiling, and grateful for the chance to witness such a thing. The risks and the dangers haven't changed, the only difference is the men's perceptions. In the book, <u>The Power</u>, by Rhonda Byrne, it is stated that a rainbow and a thunderstorm are neither good nor bad, they are just a rainbow and a thunderstorm. Our feelings are what determine if they are good or bad.

This is the strength in the Paddle of Perspective. It's not made to move us quickly through the turbulent waters; instead it allows us to adopt a more positive and meaningful view of the conditions along the way. This, in turn, makes it easier to use the other paddles to laugh, to celebrate, to have hope and confidence, to be thankful, and to love. But the most magical part of the perspective paddle isn't how it helps us through the storms, but what it teaches us to take away from them.

For me, the perspective I gained from being slap dab in the middle of major adversity has left me with a deeper appreciation for life. Being forced to learn quickly what really matters has a way of making the trivial problems seem hardly worth thinking about even once, much less twice. It seems that all too often we get our panties in a wad over things that we won't even remember tomorrow. How often have you grumbled over an extra long time while on hold, a hassle with the credit card machine, a traffic snarl, a computer glitch, an overcooked steak, someone taking the parking spot you wanted, or a misplaced book, just to name a few?

I've had some of the sweetest people apologize to me for their involvement in these types of "problems," a cashier, a nurse, a waitress, a phone operator. Let me share with you my standard reply to their thoughtful apologies. It was about ten years ago, right after a certain stormy period in my life, when I adopted this philosophy. My response to them is a heartfelt, "Don't worry about it. If this is the worst thing that I have to worry about today, then when I lay my head down on my pillow tonight, I need to tell God thank you." I challenge you to judge the events of your day using this method. If that "problem" is your biggest worry, do you really have something to complain about? Now, if you just like being fussy or miserable, don't try this because if you do, life will suddenly seem less stressful and you will end up finding more magical moments than you ever thought possible.

One of my most memorable and heartfelt lessons on how to use this paddle came from a child. Imagine that? One spring afternoon some of the kids from the neighborhood were over at our house, including two sisters and their younger brother. I told them to help themselves to something to drink and a snack from the pantry. As I walked into the kitchen to put a glass in the sink, I noticed one of the sweet girls, standing at the pantry, her hand on its open door. She was just staring inside, her gaze going from one shelf to the next. I heard her say, as much to herself as me, "Gosh, I sure wish our pantry looked like this with all of this stuff." Just the night before, I had mentioned to Terry that I had to get to the store soon because we were out of everything and there was hardly anything in the pantry; I had yet to make it there. I often think of my sweet young friend before complaining of what I don't have. Yes, the Paddle of Perspective can be a powerful tool when it comes to how we view the clouds overhead.

The world would be a much happier place if we all had this paddle out just a little more often. But sometimes understanding what a difference our perspective can make is an advantage that those of us who have encountered true adversity have over those who have not. We have been given the chance to learn the lessons that challenges teach us. My different storms have given me reasons to ask God for the resources to pay just that one bill. I have signed divorce papers. I have waited for results. I know what it feels like to pray before you go to sleep that you will wake up in the morning to hug your children once more. I've learned that sitting across the table from your spouse for a long-awaited dinner date at your favorite restaurant can be so precious that you wouldn't be upset if they brought out a hot dog instead of the steak you ordered.

This paddle has also shown me that sometimes our unexpected problems are really blessings that we just haven't recognized yet. I've found out that the irritating traffic jam on an already frustrating day is an opportunity to listen to a song with uplifting lyrics that makes you feel better about more than just the traffic. A misplaced book can provide a lesson on pulling together as a family and helping each other out. That unexpected wait at the doctor's office can give you a few uninterrupted, quiet moments that your child may need to talk to you about something that is bothering or worrying her. A change in the television schedule that keeps you from getting to watch your favorite show just might mean that, while flipping through the channels, you run across something that's helpful to you. Sometimes we need to stop and consider that those dark clouds that we blame for ruined plans and rough days are what forced us to take shelter and kept us from getting burned by the sun.

By holding the Paddle of Perspective, we can

see how often things have a way of coming together and working out. Have you been looking for Mrs. Right and feel like giving up because you haven't found her yet? For just a minute, stop to consider that your Mrs. Right might be currently gaining a new perspective on life so that she will be ready for you and the lifelong love you will share? Terry had been burned one time too many and he was at the point that he didn't want to date anyone. He says that he was just fed up and "through with it." Across town, during those same months, I was discovering the hard way what marriage shouldn't be like, how divorce proceedings worked, and what I really wanted in a husband. Through our own hardships, we each gained a perspective that I credit for the nineteen years of love and happiness that we have shared. Out of our storms came two dreams fulfilled.

Are you struggling financially? Have you lost your job? Are you drowning in debt and worry? Are you thinking, "Perspective? All I see are bills, all I want to perceive is hope." Several years ago, Terry and his brother decided that it was time to part ways, for both personal and business reasons, and Terry quit working at Steve's company after twelve years there. We decided to open our own business, but things didn't go as we had hoped and we were forced to close it. The economy being in shambles made finding another career choice extremely challenging and savings were used to live off of. It went quickly. Adversity had found us once more. So along with our other paddles, we pulled out the Paddle of Perspective. Not knowing where the currents were taking us, we had to focus on where they had brought us. The business had failed, but opening it had caused us to move from one side of town to another. We now live a mile from my parents and in the same subdivision with my beloved grandmother who needs more assistance now. I'm her only granddaughter and have always been very close to her. For years I've dreamed of living near her, especially as she got older. The failed business made that possible.

Being out of money and struggling financially stinks, but we have learned even more about relying on faith and that God will give us what we need when we need it. Not working outside of the house has allowed Terry to spend time with his children as he never has before, and he and I get to share our nights and our days with each other. Life holds no guarantees that we will ever have the chance to do this again, so for now, while we are blessed to be able to enjoy it, it is a gift. The "free time" that our adversities have brought about have allowed us the chance to pursue our passions and our hearts' callings. And isn't that what we are really here to do? Out of this storm has come more opportunities for happiness than we ever had before. I will be grateful when the skies are a clear blue, when the water is smooth, and when our boat isn't bouncing around each and every day, but I will also be shouting, "Thank you!" to the dark clouds as the sweet breezes of fortune and destiny blow them away.

So what is your current situation offering to

you? Are there doors to open that you haven't noticed or tried? Have you discovered faith and found that true happiness has no dollar signs in front of it? If not, maybe it's time to put your Paddle of Perspective in the water and find out what you've been missing. It can help you see the challenges as blessings, the currents as a means of transportation, and the storms as opportunities. Perspective is what will determine whether you emerge from your adversity a bitter or a better person. Perspective is what will decide if the storm takes from you or if you receive from it. Perspective is what gives you reasons to say, "Thank you for today!" as you lay your head on your pillow each and every night.

30

The Paddle of Action

"What we think or what we know or what we believe is, in the end, of little consequence. The only thing of consequence is what we do."
- John Ruskin

The Paddle of Action is, in many ways, the most important and most powerful of all. While it is of little use to us by itself, it is the driving force and the energy behind all of the other paddles. In order to overcome our adversities, not to merely survive them or manage to just pull through, but to come away feeling as though we have conquered the storm, we must use this paddle concurrently with the other ones.

It is our paddling equivalent to electricity. You can place a hundred lamps in a darkened room and the room will remain just as dark until an electrical current powers the lights. The same is true with our paddles. It doesn't matter how many wonderful tools you have in your boat, if they are just laying there, then they are of absolutely no benefit to you. You can understand the concept, the function, and the meaning behind each one, but until you put them into the water and start taking action with them, they won't get you anywhere.

The Paddle of Action can be used in various forms. It can be action in the physical sense, as in actually driving to and then walking around the nursing home to show love. Or it might need to take on an emotional, mental, or even intellectual nature as when we are using it with the paddles of hope, fear, and perspective. But whatever form it's in, the instructions for it are the same, and they are short and sweet- don't worry about knowing how, just start paddling with it now!

We have a tendency to put things off, usually because it seems as though the task will be easier to do later, we aren't confident in our abilities, or we are worried about the outcome. I've seen great ideas not come to fruition because they were never acted on. I know people who are stuck under the clouds simply because they won't try something new, different, or uncomfortable. I've watched magical moments slip right by because someone didn't think that the conditions were perfect.

Well, there are several problems with that kind of reasoning. First, there is no guarantee that anything will be easier later. As I have learned through life's unpredictabilities, you might find that it will only get harder if you wait. Over the years that I've spent in sales, I've come up with something that I use to persuade myself into making a phone call that I'm nervous about. I simply say to myself, "They are no more likely to say yes tomorrow than they are today, so let's go ahead and get this over with." I have found that it works for all kinds of situations that are tempting to postpone. No matter what the action is that you need or want to take, try telling yourself, "It's not likely to be any easier tomorrow than it is today, so let's just go ahead and get this over with." And, hey, if it would have been easier tomorrow, you'll never know it anyway.

As far as our abilities go, if you need or want to do something that is meaningful, to yourself or to others, the only real way that you can mess it up is to not do it at all. And the only way to get more comfortable doing something is through practice and experience. Again, are you operating off the misconception that you will wake up tomorrow and feel at ease doing that which you are nervous about today? Come on!

Here is another huge secret that I will let you in on, although it can be hard for us to accept because deep down we really wish it wasn't true. But if you will keep it in mind, you might find it easier to take action. The reality of life is that most people don't care as much about what we do or how we do it as we fear they will. And if your actions are noticed, what gets people's attention the quickest is not what we do, but the attitude it is done with.

Worrying prematurely about how something will turn out and then basing our decisions on that worry does nothing to guarantee the outcome of the situation. It only prevents us from having the chance to experience the joy of "success" and magical moments. Several years back, Ansley was very upset after losing a Student Council officer election. Having lost elections myself, I was all too familiar with her disappointment, but I also knew we were standing at the brink of a very important life-lesson. "Oh, Ans," I said, holding her close to me, "I know how upsetting this is. You wanted this position so badly and you campaigned so hard for it." After a few minutes of just being upset with her and for her, I said, "There is one way that I can guarantee that you will never lose another election or feel this way again,"

I paused as she looked up and asked, "How?"

"Just don't ever run in one again." I let it sink in, then continued, "Of course, it will also guarantee that you won't ever win one either, but if you want to be sure, that's how to do it." I got a hint of a smile. If we want to get anywhere that's worth getting to, we must take action and we must take some risks.

For those of you who are waiting for the conditions to be perfect before using those paddles, be aware that you could be sitting in the storm for a very long time, either twiddling your thumbs or hanging on for dear life, depending on your adversity. There will always be some reason that can be used to make it seem better to wait before acting, something that might improve if given some time. But at some point, you must realize that what will cause conditions to improve the quickest is for you to start paddling. The right circumstances shouldn't make us act; we should act to make the circumstances right.

Sometimes the problem can be that we get so caught up in the storm at hand that we aren't sure how to start paddling? Does your adversity have you so paralyzed with emotions that you wish you could start rowing with even one of the aforementioned paddles, but you don't know which one to grab or where to start? Your understanding of them as you are reading is one thing, your being able to use them as you are living might be another. Okay, then pay attention, because this part is specifically for you. I'll walk you through this by giving you an action plan. It's elementary, but it will get you started. You can do as many of these steps as you want at one time, but you need to do at least one each day.

The first thing to do is to get a piece of paper and a pen. Write down a name for or a description of your storm. This can be a word or two or use it as a chance to vent. If you're battling more than one, pick the one that you would make disappear first if you could just snap your fingers to do so. Done? Then guess what? You just started rowing with the Paddle of Action. You're on your way!

Next, go back to Chapter 20 on awareness and, if you haven't already done so, answer the questions I posed about your storm. I would recommend that you write the answers down on your paper so that you have to really think about them and not just skim over the words. At the very least, say your answers out loud. Your next task is to do the same with the Paddle of Hope, followed by the Paddle of Fear.

After that, pick any of the remaining paddles. Start with the one that excites you, or save it for last and get your least favorite over with, or you can "eeny-meeny-miny-moe" it. Just choose a "paddle of the day" and complete one or more of the suggested actions in that chapter. Don't make it too hard or it will seem overwhelming. Let someone pull out in front of you, celebrate a good cup of coffee, or write down three things that you are thankful for. Continue doing at least one of these a day until you have gone through them all. My guess is that you will catch yourself repeating yesterday's activity in addition to today's, because it made you feel good and we are naturally drawn to things that make us feel better.

If you use one paddle each day, by the time you have used each one, you will have spent a week actively paddling through your storm. Not bad for someone who felt paralyzed and didn't know where to start. Keep it up! Now can you see the light shining through the clouds?

The power of this paddle and one of the main ways that it helps us navigate through life's storms is that taking action gives us more control. After being sick, I could have sat on the sofa and done nothing but rest. And it would have gotten me nowhere. Yes, my body might have been well rested, but the storm would have only intensified. I needed to take action with any and all of my paddles to overcome my adversity because for me, as is true with so many who are struggling with health issues, my greatest fight wasn't for my physical well-being. It was the battle for who I would see in the mirror after the storm.

Many times one of my concerned family members has said to me in response to something I've decided to do or to some activity or project that I've taken on, "You don't have to push yourself. There will be other chances for you to do that. Take it easy." As far as not needing to push myself goes, they are wrong. When I am fighting my way through one of life's storms, I do need to push myself. It is when the currents are the roughest that it takes more effort to get us to where we need and want to go. It is by pushing and challenging ourselves that we will gain more control and be better able to get out from under the thunderheads. So, if I don't want to complain, then I'd better act.

As for my family members telling me that there will be other chances to do those things, I know the odds are that they're right. But my experiences have made me all too aware that there is a real possibility that another chance may never come to pass. And if it does, it will just give me a second opportunity to do something that I think is important, and I can decide then whether to take action or not.

But for today, even if it's something that we're not chomping at the bit to tackle, but we think needs to be done, then let's do it! We usually end up feeling better for having taken action, and often the action brings with it fun or meaningful experiences that can change our outlook for the whole day and beyond. So why are we waiting?

It's not going to be any easier tomorrow, right?

Let's flip the switch and get power running to our paddles. Ask yourself what are you rowing towards and what would make you smile? Once you know why, decide on an action to get your paddles moving in the right direction. It doesn't have to be big, but start acting instead of waiting. Make the phone call, get what you need from the store, look up something online. But get to it because once you notice that those storm clouds seem to be moving, you'll be glad you did.

Are you looking for that someone special to share life with? The odds are that he or she isn't going to parachute into your yard. Most likely you are going to have to paddle towards that person. Hopefully he or she will be coming towards you at the same time. There are all kinds of action that you can take with this situation. Let friends know you're looking, join a singles group, or, bite the bullet, and ask out that person you've had your eye on, to name a few.

Or you can try what I did. Tell God that you are leaving it up to Him this time, but that you are ready and open when He sends you Mr. Right. I went on to list things that I thought I wanted in a man, if it was okay with God of course. Two weeks later, Terry asked me out. He has every single quality that I had listed. We believe that God put us together, but it took action and risk on both of our parts to make it happen. What if I hadn't been open or figured that it was too soon so it must be too good to be true? What if Terry decided that it wasn't worth the risk of getting hurt again and hadn't asked me out? Thank you, God, for sending Terry to me. And thank you, Sweetheart, for being willing to take action, and thank you for every day that we've shared since!

Are you having a hard time in school? I'm going to tell you to take the obvious action of studying. But there might be something more going on, and if so you know that better than anyone. I've been there, but I didn't know what action to take, so I'm telling you what to do. Paddle yourself straight into the counselor's office and say this, "I need some help." If for some reason that doesn't do the trick, I'm going to recommend calling a local preacher again. You don't even have to know him or her. Just say, "My name is ____. I'm __ years old. I talked to the counselors at school, but it didn't help, and I don't know who else to ask. Can you help me find a tutor (or a mentor, or someone to talk to)?" And my advice remains the same- if you don't get what you need, hang up and call another pastor. Listen, most preachers have good hearts, but that doesn't mean they are all good pastors. I'm a preacher's kid; I can say it.

Are you struggling with losing someone? Maybe the action you need to take is to write down your feelings. No, it doesn't have to be an eloquent poem. If you're mad, scribble mean, nasty words as hard as you can all over a piece of paper, and then rip it to shreds! There! If the loss was through a death, the action you need to take might be calling to get information on a support group, going through a closet, or asking a friend to come sit with you while you look at pictures or watch a video.

If it's loneliness that you are battling, attend a group function. It doesn't have to be the best time of your life, the purpose is just to put you in contact with other people. Or get out your address book, find the number of an old friend, and call just to say hello.

All of these suggestions have one thing in common, you taking action, which is often the way that we can emerge from a storm feeling positive. Paddling with action allows life to happen through us, not to us.

One of the most beautiful things about this special paddle is that by using it we can often help others while helping ourselves. Are you trying to get your mind off of a problem? Is there a senior citizen who needs help filling out her tax return? Make the offer. Are you in need of more physical exercise and the neighbor, the one you heard broke his leg in an accident, needs his grass cut? I've got a crazy idea. Are you coping with empty nest syndrome and the young couple at church has a little one, no family in town, and is probably struggling financially? Pick up your action and compassion paddles on a Saturday night and babysit for free to give them a little time together. Is your marriage in a rut? Maybe telling your spouse how much he means to you, that your love is unconditional, and that you just plain like him would help. I can't think of a better time than right now. Put the book down, grab this paddle and the Paddle of Love and go tell him! If he isn't around, the moment he walks in the door will work just fine. Does your child need to know that you are so proud of her for how hard she studied for that science test, and that the grade she ends up with is second compared to the effort that she put out? Brag on her to someone else where she can hear or post a message on her Facebook page, but be sure to also tell her in person. Has your other child been asking to do something with you? Maybe he wants to play a game, go on a walk, bake brownies, or let you listen to his new favorite song. You've been meaning to, but time has a way of slipping by. Here's the solution- act now. Do it today!

Finding out how unpredictable life can be has taught me that if it is worth doing, then it's worth not putting off. If it will make a difference in your life or in the life of someone else, then make the time, take the risk, and act. It won't always seem like it's worth the effort and some things can be uncomfortable and hard, but the Paddle of Action has a way of creating magical moments that will come back around to find us. Action is the force that moves us to that place where we can honestly and eagerly say, "Thank you for today and for how far I've come!" Then, as we sit amazed at the progress we have made and contemplating what action to take next, we may happen to glance upwards and be surprised to find that we were too busy doing to notice that the storm has passed.

31

The Ongoing Pursuit of the Sun

"What lies behind us and what lies before us are small matters compared to what lies within us."
- Ralph Waldo Emerson

    The flow of life has taken me through not only those major storms that I have shared with you, but many others as well. There have been heartbreaks, problems at school, job issues, betrayal, troubles with family relationships, bad decisions and tough choices. Most of these other storms have long since dissipated, but some of the consequences from them will be with me forever. Others are an ongoing battle and hover endlessly overhead, requiring me to keep my paddles close by and not allowing me to raise the sails just yet.

    One of the toughest and most emotional of those lingering fronts started a couple of years after Faith was born. Terry and I had decided that it was time for child number three. Ever since we were dating, both of us had wanted at least three children. I was feeling much better and stronger and was off all medications. When the doctors gave us the go-ahead to get pregnant, we were thrilled! We celebrated by trading in my much-loved car for a minivan. The excitement didn't last long. No one could have predicted the trouble that we would have, but we experienced one miscarriage after another. The doctors said that my past medical history had nothing to do with them. It was more a factor of age; I was thirty-six.

My predisposition for not doing anything the easy way was proven when the first miscarriage happened on Ansley's birthday. Not wanting to ruin her day or her party, I didn't make a big deal about it, which was fairly easy to do since I had only known for a couple of days that I was expecting. My prayer whenever I was pregnant had always been for "a happy, healthy baby." With my Paddle of Perspective in hand, I knew that a miscarriage meant something was wrong and maybe this was the answer to that prayer. The second miscarriage was more emotional as I was near the end of my first trimester. We were on the way to Disney World with my dad and stepmom where we celebrated Faith's fourth birthday. There's nothing like trying to hide the blood from your seven and four year olds in a hotel room and being forced to choose between lying flat in the room or putting down the Paddle of Hope and joining them in their fun. An ultrasound at the local hospital made the decision for me as it showed us that the baby wasn't alive. Using all of the paddles, but especially those of love, laughter, and celebration, helped me to enjoy the rest of the trip. Then, six months later, on Ansley's next birthday, another pregnancy came to an end. This time we were visiting Matt and his wife, Emily, in New York. All I wanted was my bed to curl up in. Instead, I pulled out the paddles again and we coped with the disappointment. It might seem that the miscarriages were related to the travel or the excitement of birthday celebrations except that there were others in between and after those. Finally, Terry and I took out our Paddle of Gratitude and said to each other and to God, "We have two healthy and happy girls who are incredibly beautiful, inside and out. We are so blessed and thankful. We're good."

I meant it, but there was a part of me that just couldn't let go. I always thought that no matter what the doctors said, there was some connection between my illness and the miscarriages. Perhaps my body just wasn't strong enough or maybe it had something to do with my nerves. I don't know. I just remember countless times when either a pregnancy had ended or when my period had started that I would cry and beg, "Please! That stupid disease took so much away from me. Please not this too. It's not fair!" This storm was different than the others. It wasn't threatening; it was sad. I never put down my Paddle of Hope, but I didn't really know how to use it either as there wasn't any action that I could take to change this. And life went on.

Most of the time I would let life's currents

determine my daily course. I found that in doing so the days can sometimes be exhausting, sometimes refreshing, and usually a combination of crazy and comforting. But, oh, the beautiful blessings and the happiness that I discovered along the way. I remember one Fourth of July when the four of us went to see a large fireworks display that is an annual tradition for us. We made our way through the massive crowds, found our customary spot, and laid down together on the blanket that we spread over the pavement. As the fireworks began exploding in front of us, Terry and I interlocked fingers above the two little heads, one with blonde hair, one with brunette, separating us. For a moment, we took our attention away from the cascading lights to look at the spectacular sight of our girls just lying there mesmerized and to smile at each other. I remember thinking, "Things are exactly as they are supposed to be, right here and right now." I teared up at this magical moment that I was in the middle of. Yes, life's currents have a way of taking us to beautiful places.

Today they had me at the kitchen table playing a family board game and listening to the squeals of a two-and-a-half-year-old informing her older sisters that they were not Mommy's babies, she was! Like I said, some of the things that come out of our storms stay with us forever. On June 6, 2008, Kylee Marie Kasha was born, and our family and my heart were finally complete. This surprise pregnancy happened a year and a half after my last miscarriage and we had no problems whatsoever with it. I've stated on more than one occasion that I just carried Kylee as a surrogate because my baby really belongs to her older, doting sisters and to her daddy. She is a gorgeous, bubbly, happy, and healthy little girl, full of questions and love. And she has shown us all that some of life's most beautiful and precious gifts are worth the wait.

The ironic part of Kylee's story is that the paddle that I believe made the difference in bringing her into our lives wasn't intended for her. I got pregnant not long after we had returned from our family vacation to the Southwestern United States. I related how I wanted Ansley and Faith to come home with wonderful memories. So I used the Paddle of Hope to help me build up my strength by walking when I didn't feel up to it. I will always wonder how much increasing my endurance and getting stronger affected the healthy pregnancy. And that Peachtree Road Race that I was training for, but never ran, it was Miss Kylee that caused my change of plans. Well, there will be other races, but there's only one Kylee. And with her energy level, I'm now in training every day. Yes, the race can wait, but life and the blessings that can come from the storms won't. I wonder if some of the paddles you have pulled out to tackle one problem might end up bringing you relief from other storms and gifts that you aren't expecting.

Although waiting can be hard, no matter how old we are, there is an appreciation for what we don't get easily that adds a little something special to it. At night, as I am rocking Kylee and singing her favorite lullabies, I often look at her and say,

"Mommy sure did wait a long time for you, Baby! I love you so much, Kylee!"

Then that tiny little face with those big eyes will look up at me in the glow of the hallway light and say, "I love you too, Mommy."

And I know that I'd go through that storm all over again to get to where I am right now. I know now what I was waiting for. As I rock back and forth, with my arms wrapped around the love that's snuggled against me, I am thankful to have "just one more song" requested so that I don't have to end this treasured time, a magical moment that I almost gave up hope of ever happening. Kylee giggles at the sound of a train running past our neighborhood and I look out the window and notice the moon shining through the trees. Glancing towards the sky, I smile and say, "Thank you for this! Thank you for today!"

She can't understand it yet, but someday I will explain to my daughter that our family needed her as much as she needed us. Kylee's birth came in the middle of winds blowing at us from every direction and waves that just kept coming, one after another. She gave us something beautiful and wonderful to focus our attention on and offered us a distraction from the rough waters that were churning all around. In the last half of 2007, we got out our paddles and haven't had the chance to put them down since. And yes, there have been many times when Terry and I have wondered just how much more we can take. It isn't that we don't have faith that we'll make it through these trying times, it's just that it would be nice to have a chance to catch our breath before the next round hits.

To begin with, we were hit with a crash course in the politics that can take place even in the best of churches, like ours. After that storm ended, we were taken by surprise when it came to light that some members of Terry's family were having strained feelings towards me regarding the way I had handled conflicts that arose between us, and the differences of opinion we have involving some moral, social, and religious issues. They were also concerned about some of Terry's decisions and actions. Because we were dealing with strong emotional topics, it made it hard to have productive discussions. The pain that this unexpected adversity caused came not as much from their feelings towards me, but from watching my husband suffer over being judged so unfairly and being stuck in the middle, forced to choose between his loyalties to the people he loves. Seeing this wonderful man, who had given so much to me, to his children, to the church, and to countless others, now hurting so badly was as agonizing as anything else that I had gone through. It wasn't easy and it took a lot of paddling, but we were able to come away from the turbulence with his family agreeing to disagree and perhaps with a better understanding of each other. There were days when it didn't seem to be going in that direction, but Terry and I also came away from the experience finding that our marriage and relationship was even stronger than it had been before.

Not long after that was when Terry and his brother decided to part ways with work. It was the right decision, but it led us to discover the challenges that job hunting can bring. Around that same time is when we found out that I was expecting Kylee. Holding our breaths, we kept marking off the days, weeks, and months of the pregnancy that passed with no problems. By the time we were able to relax, the decision had been made, largely due to the lack of desired results from the job search, to open our own business. This prompted our move to the other side of town and the decision to rent out our current home. Someone could make a reality television show from the experience of meeting with and checking out interested tenants. The final result has worked out beautifully. We laugh as we recall that it came about, not as a response to our ads, but because, as the family was in our neighborhood to look at another house for rent, they just happened to drive by ours and saw our sign. They stopped and asked if they could have a look. I thank God that they had their Paddles of Action out and called from the car because now my beloved house, that was always filled with the spirit of laughter and love and that serves as the backdrop for so many treasured memories, is now the home to another family and their joy and magical moments together.

A few months later during the first part of June, in the wee hours of a Friday morning, our beautiful baby was born. I cried countless tears of joy as my perfect, healthy little girl was laid against my bare skin. Many loving arms were waiting to hold her, but they all had to get in line behind Faith and Ansley. Terry and I smiled at each other and held hands as we watched love come alive in front of us. It may have been dark outside, but the sun was shining brightly in that hospital room and those storm clouds that had been looming over us for so long were nowhere to be seen.

I don't seem to be able to do anything the easy way. Kylee was born on Friday, we took her home on Sunday, and then moved into our new home on Tuesday. We had started the new business out of the house, but were moving into a nearby warehouse that Terry had renovated. In August, we opened to the public, just a couple of weeks after Ansley and Faith had started at their new schools. On top of everything else, we were literally in mourning over leaving behind the church that had been such a major part of our lives for fifteen years.

A friend of the family jokingly said that Terry and I should just go ahead and file for divorce, since the leading factors of marriage troubles are a new baby, a job change, loss of income, and a major move. Since we thought that we would take them all on at once, why not get the inevitable divorce over with? Yes, Terry and I were exhausted physically, emotionally, mentally, and financially. But as the winds tried to blow us off course and the currents threatened to drag us under, we just dug our paddles in deeper and pushed harder, especially that Paddle of Love.

And there, in the midst of the storms, we discovered just what a blessing our marriage is.

One would think that we were due a break, but keep in mind that the further off shore you travel, the greater the adventures and the risks will be. I was starting to think that we had found a riptide and I couldn't remember the last time we had seen land. Our paddles might have been worn, but we were learning that they were still strong.

This proved to be true as that ugly Paddle of Awareness was needed to make the final decision to close down our business two years after opening it. It was time to face the fact that it wasn't going to be as profitable as we had hoped, and the hole we were in was only getting deeper. Then, as savings dwindled and resumes were sent out, we gained tremendous experience in how to use the Paddle of Hope. Often it was needed just to get to the next day, to pay the next bill, to make the next decision. Terry and I discovered that the Paddle of Confidence can be extremely difficult to hold, much less to dig in, when what we attempted didn't work out and the risks we took hadn't paid off. The blame might lay with the economy, the industry, or our actions, but no matter its source, some things come back around to fall onto your shoulders. And when something you tried isn't successful, there is nothing that feels good about it, and afterwards having confidence can seem next to impossible. But if Terry and I were going to move forward and get to where we wanted to be, we needed to dig deep inside ourselves to find the strength to pick up that paddle. Of course that meant that we would need to take action at the very time when we just wanted a break, especially an emotional one.

But the Paddles of Gratitude and Perspective were there to keep us going. And they have been needed as I once again found myself under dark clouds. And once more, I also have reasons to be grateful as another miracle blew into my life with one more storm.

Last January, Ansley and Faith had just started back to school after the Christmas break. Tuesday morning, Ansley sent me a text message while she was on the school bus. It said, "not going to be a good day. I can already tell." I still have it saved on my phone. She wasn't the only one feeling down. I thought that just getting out of the house might lift my spirits, so I loaded up Kylee in the van and went to fill up with gas and get my comforting cappuccino from the closest QuikTrip. Headed home, I had just left one of the county's busiest roads and was getting ready to cross another one when I decided to stop at a sandwich shop to grab some lunch for us. Realizing that I had come in at a bad angle to pull into the open parking spaces, I exited back onto the street to try again using a different entrance.

I pulled carefully out of the parking lot and then opened my eyes to find myself in the back of an ambulance. The rig's back doors were open and I was looking at the heavy flow of traffic on the road that I had exited onto. I was told that I had had a seizure. Ten years after the encephalitis with no incidents, something had triggered one. Kylee was in the ambulance beside me and was okay, but I wasn't, at least not emotionally. "No!" I thought, horrified and in shock. "No, no, no!"

It happened as I was pulling back into the parking lot. The van's wheels were angled just right so that I ran up onto a grassy embankment, stopping just short of the sandwich shop's brick side wall. I barely missed a concrete drainage box on one side and a metal pole on the other. Some men working on telephone wires saw what happened. When I didn't get out, they called 911. Thank you, Gentlemen! The van was still in drive when the paramedics arrived. They placed Kylee, still buckled in her car seat, in the ambulance with me.

Terry was called and he met us before they took me to the hospital. He called my parents and they came to get Kylee. Words will never be able to express how sorry I am for the heart-stopping phone calls that my family has received about me. The agony those calls must have caused is almost more than I can handle and the pain and horror my little girls have had to endure breaks my heart.

Then come the what-if's. Chills run down my back, and my stomach and throat tighten when I think of what could have happened if that seizure had occurred at any moment other than the second it did. Yes, miracles often come in the form of moments that happen during the course of our days, and gratitude can be found in the strangest places. I see it in a parking lot on a little patch of grass every time we drive by.

The doctor said that the stars were just aligned

for the seizure to happen. Because of the lesions on my brain, I'll always be at more of a risk, so he put me on anti-seizure medicine. I wasn't at all thrilled with the idea of being on medication for the rest of my life, bu then I picked up the Paddle of Perspective and realized what it was trying to show me.

I had been on anti-seizure medicine after my illness, but had weaned off of it per my doctor's instructions after tests showed that my risk for seizures was very low. The reason I had wanted to get off of it was because it shouldn't be taken unless absolutely necessary while pregnant. And I wanted another baby. Well, I got my baby and I got to nurse her without any risks.

No, I wish I didn't have to be on medication and I wish that I had some guarantee of no more seizures, but that not being the case, I see that the timing allowed me to have what mattered the most to me and there couldn't have been a better outcome from this situation. No one was hurt, Faith and Ansley were at school and didn't see anything that would have traumatized them, Kylee was too young to know the difference, and there was no damage to any property or to the van. After doing some research, I found out that I had unknowingly combined several seizure trigger factors in the twenty-four hours prior to this happening. I would have preferred a different method of learning that combining intense stress, hormones, alcohol, a lack of sleep, and over-the-counter medicine is not a good idea if you have a history of seizures. Now I know. All in all, I really don't have much to complain about. The Paddle of Perspective has helped me see a horrible storm as something miraculous, and I feel so thankful and blessed!

There have been other fronts that we have come through and others still ahead of us. It's called life. At our wedding Terry sang a song that he wrote for me, titled "Not Enough." In it are the words, "I want you here beside me every minute of this roller coaster ride." Not long ago he clarified that when he wrote those words, he had been thinking more in terms of the fun, exciting kiddie coasters, not the Goliath death-defying ones.

Sorry, Sweetheart. But I probably wouldn't pack those paddles away just yet if I were you. We've got many horizons left to reach and I'm guessing that we will be using them a lot to get there. And one day, as we look back, I have a feeling that we will see that it was in using our paddles together that we found meaning, purpose, and joy in our journey. Hey, look out there in front of us! Is that the sunshine sparkling on the water? Grab the girls and let's go see!

32

The Gifts

*"Life is a gift, and it offers us
the privilege, opportunity, and responsibility
to give something back by becoming more."*
- Tony Robbins

    I'm still here, sitting close to my computer screen, continuing to type with my now-tough right index finger. I have been too busy reliving and recounting my journey to think much about my back hurting or the nagging ache in my shoulder. They'll be fine. At one point I did decide that I should try using both hands on the keyboard, typing the way I used to be able to. I was never fast, but I was decent. Now if I use the correct fingering positions, it means having to go back and correct a mistake in every other word. Practice is a very effective form of therapy, so I attempted to retrain myself, thinking that writing would go faster and be more comfortable for one busy finger and one not so uselful hand. But I quickly discovered how inefficient trying to be efficient can be. I had to concentrate so hard on making my fingers hit the right keys that I couldn't pay attention to what my spirit was telling me to say. I definitely wasn't getting anywhere faster, except frustrated. Maybe someday I'll try again with a more prolonged effort, but for now more important things beckon my attention. I need to focus on and use what I can do and not waste time on what I can't. Whether I'm typing with one finger, two hands, or my toes, there is still a story to tell and a message to share.

I think back to what I said at the beginning of this book about how I wished the letters I've been staring at could tell me specifically what message I should share. While writing this, I have found myself bouncing back and forth between smiles, tears, disbelief, and wonder, and I realize that perhaps the letters have done just that. By traveling back over my own journey, one thought, one memory, one word, and one letter at a time, I have been able to see a message that's been hiding amongst the waves and beneath the clouds:

*Our lives are a matter of perspective,
our journeys a matter of perception.
It's not the storms that give meaning to our lives,
it's our lives that give meaning to the storms.*

When struggling with adversity, we often want to examine it, hoping to recognize some reason, some worthwhile purpose, some greater plan for why this has happened to us. But we are only wasting our time, for what we seek can't be found in the storms that blow our way. Instead, the answers are waiting to be discovered inside each of us. They are in our own awareness, in our hopes, our fears, and in the confidence that we find in ourselves. The answers will be seen in our celebrations and heard in our laughter. Our own unique messages will be written through our compassion and displayed by our gratitude. And they will be felt and passed along in the ways that we recognize and show love and in the actions that we choose to take.

When my friend, Gale, asked me how I manage to stay so positive with everything that I have gone through, I didn't have an answer. So we joked that either I'm crazy enough to not know the difference or that by now I just figure, "Hey, what's one more thing?" But the message above revealed something to me. The answer, my sweet friend, would have to be simply that I have learned that life is what we make of it. I may not have a say in which storms I encounter, but I do have a choice in their outcomes. So, for as long as I am able, I will choose for my journey to be filled with beauty, meaning, fun, magical moments, joy, and love. Often I look towards the heavens, searching for guidance, comfort, and reassurance. And when I do, it isn't that I don't see the threatening clouds above me, notice those in front of me, or recall the ones from my past. It is just that I have come to understand that behind every one of those ominous-looking clouds, no matter how dark or threatening it may seem, the sun is still shining brightly. But it is up to me to paddle to a place where its light and warmth can be seen, felt, and enjoyed.

No, I can't stop the storms and neither can you.

And sometimes life does just plain suck. But how you and I row through our adversities, what we take from them, and the messages we discover in them, those are our choices. I don't know where life's currents will end up taking me and I'm well aware that the course I planned today may change tomorrow. But for now, my focus is on the next horizon. Once I get there, I'll see what lies beyond that. All of my paddles are out and within reach. They are ready to be used at a moment's notice, for come what may, they'll be needed. That I can guarantee.

It would certainly make things simpler if we had some type of "life radar" that would allow us to prepare for what lies ahead and to see what's coming our way. But that's not how this trip works. And besides, what fun would that be?

Each day of our lives is a gift that we have been given, complete with its own joys and troubles, as it is with anything of value. While we might not know what today will bring, keep in mind that gifts you have to unwrap before finding out what's inside have a magic about them that expected presents will never possess. It is the element of surprise and the not knowing that intrigues and excites us. If only we felt that way about many of life's gifts.

We need to understand that the joy of receiving a present isn't really in the present itself, but in the recipient's reaction to it. But because many of life's most majestic gifts don't come in beautiful wrappings, we are quick to assume that they're of little worth to us and that they won't bring anything good into our lives. If we would only accept and unwrap each one with the understanding that we can't always appreciate how priceless and special something really is until much later, when we can see the positive impact that it has had on our lives. Too often we get impatient and immediately feel resentful or cheated by what we got or didn't get. We aren't open enough to stop and take the time to look at what we are holding from different perspectives. And that can cause us to miss out on the messages, the miracles, and the magical moments that life's storms can bring to us.

Yes, there will always be those days that seem like the kind of present that we wish had come with a receipt so that it could be returned. But still a gift it is, one with unlimited opportunities for growing, celebrating, prospering, and for making a difference in our own lives and in the lives of others. It is a gift that offers us the chance to take action, to find answers, to feel grateful, and that just might help us discover the joy that's in our journeys.

Did today bring adversity? Most likely it did, for we are on life's waters and rarely do they remain smooth for long. But with the adversity came a chance to experience hope, to understand truth, and to face fear head on. We got to play in the game, learn life's lessons, and discover that we can feel good about ourselves.

So tonight when I go to bed, after quietly walking into each of my daughters' bedrooms to give them one more kiss good night and to whisper, "I love you," and after Terry and I have exchanged the words of our treasured ritual and a kiss or two, I will take a little time before falling asleep to reflect on today's moments and life's currents. I will notice the illumination from the moon and the streetlight sneaking in through the closed blinds, as if to remind me that there are sources of light even in the darkness. Then, with a smile on my face, a tear in my eye, and gratitude in the deepest part of my heart, I will say to God, "Thank you for today! Did it go as I would have planned? No, and because it didn't, I found opportunities to comprehend real happiness, to laugh, and to feel love. So thank you, God, for the chance to truly live and to use my paddles. Thank you for the blessings that the storms blew in to me and for the vision to see them when they arrived." When I feel Terry's hand pull away from where it will have been resting on my waist as he turns to face the other way, I will smile with the understanding that some connections really can't be broken and some storms are worth paddling through.

"Hey, God, while we're at it, can I just go ahead and say, 'Thank you for tomorrow'?"

May your journey be filled with joy.

Made in the USA
Charleston, SC
13 June 2011